THE
Oneness
VIEW
of
JESUS
CHRIST

THE
Oneness
VIEW
of
JESUS
CHRIST

DAVID K. BERNARD

The Oneness View of Jesus Christ

by David K. Bernard

©1994, David K. Bernard
Printing History: 1996, 1998, 2000, 2004

Cover Design by Tim Agnew

Printed in United States of America

WORD AFLAME®PRESS
8855 DUNN ROAD
HAZELWOOD, MO 63042-2299
www.pentecostalpublishing.com

Library of Congress Cataloging-in-Publication Data
Bernard, David K., 1956—
    The oneness view of Jesus Christ / by David K. Bernard.
        p.   cm.
    Includes bibliographical references and indexes.
    ISBN 1-56722-020-7
    1. Jesus Christ–Person and offices. 2. Oneness doctrine
(Pentecostalism) 3. United Pentecostal Church International-
-Doctrines. 4. Oneness Pentecostal churches–Doctrines. I. Title.
BT202.B416   1994
232´.8–dc20   94-4416
                                                   CIP

Contents

Preface

The Oneness View of Jesus Christ is a sequel to *The Oneness of God*, published in 1983. It explores in greater depth key concepts related to the Oneness understanding of the doctrine of God as revealed in Scripture, focusing on the identity of Jesus Christ. It particularly investigates some key passages of Scripture that trinitarians often use in an attempt to refute Oneness and that offer profound insight into the nature of God and the Incarnation.

Chapter 1 was originally presented as a paper at the 1989 annual meeting of the Society for Pentecostal Studies, which was held in Fresno, California, in November of that year. The Society, of which I am a member, is a nondenominational, predominantly trinitarian organization of scholars who study the Pentecostal and charismatic movements. The paper provides an overview of the Oneness doctrine. Consequently, much of its content first appeared in previous works of mine, and there is some overlap with subsequent chapters of this book, which elaborate on many of the same points. It is included here so that the reader can obtain maximum benefit from the present volume without having to read or reread *The Oneness of God.*

Most of the other chapters have appeared as articles in the *Pentecostal Herald:* chapter 2 in December 1991, chapter 3 in December 1989, chapter 4 in April 1989, chapter 5 in June 1989, most of chapter 6 in August 1992, chapter 7 in December 1992, chapter 9 in December 1993, chapter 11 in August 1988, and appendix A in September 1988. Appendix B appeared as a book review in the April-

June 1993 issue of the *Forward* (periodical for United Pentecostal ministers) and in the Spring 1993 issue of *Pneuma* (journal of the Society for Pentecostal Studies). In some cases, slight editorial changes and additions have been made since the original publication.

The more a person studies the doctrine of God and Christ in Scripture, the more he is awed by the richness and depth of this truth. While the basic concept of the almighty God in Jesus Christ is so simple that a child can readily grasp it, the message of the Incarnation is so awesome that no scholar can exhaust its riches or plumb it depths. We can understand, believe, proclaim, and explain the truth of God's oneness and His manifestation in Christ, but we cannot pretend to know all there is to know about God.

Passages of Scripture that seem to pose a difficulty for the Oneness teaching actually yield precious insights when studied prayerfully, contextually, and in harmony with the rest of Scripture. My hope is that this book will help the reader to investigate the Word of God further, uncover exciting nuggets of truth, and obtain a fresh, clear view of Jesus Christ.

1

The Oneness View of Jesus Christ

The doctrine known as Oneness can be stated in two affirmations: (1) There is one God with no distinction of persons; (2) Jesus Christ is all the fullness of the Godhead incarnate.

According to one estimate, approximately one-fourth of American Pentecostals adhere to the Oneness view of God.[1] Moreover, throughout church history and even today many people have independently arrived at essentially the same formulation.[2] Despite the evident significance of the Oneness doctrine, however, relatively few historians or theologians have given it adequate attention.

This chapter presents the basic tenets of Oneness, focusing particularly on the Oneness view of Jesus. It seeks to present a unified, internally consistent Oneness theology that is characteristic of the movement as a whole and that specifically reflects the position expressed in the publications of the United Pentecostal Church International, the largest Oneness Pentecostal body.

I. The Oneness of God

One of the clearest themes of Scripture is an uncompromising monotheism. Simply stated, God is absolutely and indivisibly one. There are no essential distinctions in His eternal nature. All names and titles of the Deity—such as Elohim, Yahweh, Lord, Father, Word, and Holy Spirit—refer to one and the same being. Any plurality associated with God merely relates to attributes, titles, roles, manifestations, modes of activity, relationships to humanity, or aspects of God's self-revelation.

This monotheistic view is the historic position of Judaism. Both Oneness and Jewish believers find the classic expression of this belief in Deuteronomy 6:4: "Hear, O Israel: The LORD our God is one LORD." Jesus emphasized the importance of this teaching, calling it "the first of all the commandments" (Mark 12:29), and in His conversation with a Samaritan woman He endorsed the Jewish concept of God: "Ye worship ye know not what: we know what we worship: for salvation is of the Jews" (John 4:22).

Many other biblical passages affirm strict monotheism, excluding any concept of plurality in the Deity; therefore, Oneness theology holds that it is biblically incorrect to speak of God as a trinity of persons.[3]

Neither the Old Testament writers nor their audiences thought of God as a trinity. If God were essentially three, He did not reveal this concept to Israel, His chosen people, and Abraham, the father of the faithful of all ages, did not comprehend the fundamental nature of his God.

It is also important to note that the New Testament speakers and writers were monotheistic Jews who expressed no thought of introducing a dramatic new revelation of a plurality in God. Neither the writers nor the readers thought in trinitarian categories; essential trinitarian terms and ideas were not formulated in New Testament times.[4]

Neither testament uses the word *trinity* or associates the words *three* or *persons* with God in any significant way.[5] No passage says God is a holy two, holy three, or holy trinity, but over fifty verses call God the "Holy One" (Isaiah 54:5). The only New Testament passage to use the word *person (hupostasis)* in relation to God is Hebrews 1:3, which says the Son is the image of God's own person (substance). Thus the terms and concepts necessary to construct the trinitarian dogma do not appear in Scripture.

Trinitarianism is not pure monotheism; rather, it tends toward tritheism. For example, the Cappadocian fathers said that the three divine persons were one God in the same way that Peter, James, and John were all human, and this analogy is frequently used today.[6] Trinitarian art often depicts the three divine persons as three men, or as an old man, a young man, and a dove.

Many trinitarian Pentecostals are theological tritheists. Finis Dake spoke of God as "three separate persons," each one being an "individual" with his "own personal spirit body, personal soul, and personal spirit in the same sense each human being, angel or any other being has his own body, soul, and spirit. . . . The word *God* is used either as a singular or a plural word, like *sheep*." [7] Jimmy Swaggart adopted the foregoing language and further wrote, "You can think of God the Father, God the Son, and God the Holy Ghost as three different persons exactly as you would think of any three other people—their 'oneness' pertaining strictly to their being one in purpose, design, and desire."[8]

II. The Deity of Jesus Christ

Jesus Christ is the one God incarnate. "In him dwelleth all the fulness of the Godhead bodily" (Colossians 2:9). "God was in Christ, reconciling the world unto himself" (II Corinthians 5:19). Jesus accepted Thomas's confession of Him as "my Lord and my God" (John 20:28-29). And many other scriptural passages reveal the identity of Jesus as God.[9]

Jesus is God in the Old Testament sense; that is what New Testament writers meant when they called Jesus God. Trinitarians maintain that only one of three divine persons, a second person who is called "God the Son," came in flesh, but the Bible does not make such a claim; it simply says that God came in flesh. Oneness theology holds that Jesus is not the incarnation of one person of a trinity but the incarnation of all the identity, character, and personality of the one God.

Frank Stagg, a Southern Baptist seminary professor (now retired) and nominally a trinitarian, has stated this position well:

Jesus Christ is God uniquely present in a truly

human life, but he is not a second god nor only one third of God. . . . The Word which became flesh was God, not the second person of the trinity. . . . Jesus Christ is more than 'the Second person of the trinity'; He is Immanuel, God with us. Immanuel does not mean 'the Second person of the trinity with us.' Immanuel is God with us.[10]

Jesus is Yahweh. Many Old Testament statements by or about Yahweh (Jehovah) are specifically fulfilled in Jesus.[11] The Old Testament describes Yahweh as the Almighty, only Savior, Lord of lords, First and Last, only Creator, Holy One, Redeemer, Judge, Shepherd, and Light; the New Testament ascribes all these titles to Jesus Christ.

Jesus is the Father incarnate. He said, "I and my Father are one," "He that hath seen me hath seen the Father," and "The Father . . . dwelleth in me" (John 10:30; 14:9-10). The One who was born as the Son is also the everlasting Father; the Father is also the Redeemer (Isaiah 9:6; 63:16). (See also John 10:38; I John 3:1-5; Revelation 21:6-7.) The Bible attributes many of the same works both to the Father and to Jesus: resurrecting Christ's body, sending the Comforter, drawing people to God, answering prayer, sanctifying believers, and resurrecting the dead.

The Holy Spirit is literally the Spirit that was in Jesus Christ. "The Lord is the Spirit" (II Corinthians 3:17, NKJV). (See also John 14:17-18; 16:7.) The New Testament ascribes the following works both to Jesus and to the Holy Spirit: moving on prophets of old, resurrection of Christ's body, work as the Paraclete, giving of words to believers in time of persecution, intercession, sanctification, and indwelling of believers.

The Holy Spirit is the Spirit of the Son, the Spirit of Jesus Christ (Galatians 4:6; Philippians 1:19). The spirit of a man is not a different person than he, but pertains to him, or is his very essence. So it is with Jesus Christ and His Spirit. Christians do not receive three divine spirits, nor do they learn to recognize three distinct personalities; they encounter one personal spirit being.

Although a trinitarian, Lewis Smedes has essentially acknowledged this position: "In the new age, the Lord is the Spirit. . . . The Spirit is the ascended Jesus in His earthly action. . . . This suggests that we do not serve a biblical purpose by insisting on the Spirit as a person who is separate from the person whose name is Jesus."[12]

Jesus is the One on the throne in heaven. (Compare Revelation 1:7-8, 11, 17-18 with 4:2, 8.) The vision of the One on the throne and the Lamb in Revelation 5 symbolizes the Incarnation and Atonement. The One on the throne is the Deity, while the Lamb represents the Son in His human, atoning role. The Lamb actually came out of the throne and sits on the throne (Revelation 5:6; 7:17). As the lexicon of Bauer, Arndt, Gingrich and Danker states, the Lamb "is (seated) on the center of the throne."[13]

In Revelation 22:3-4, "God and the Lamb" is one being with one throne, one face, and one name. Only Jesus is both sovereign and sacrifice—deity and humanity—at the same time. He is the image of the invisible God, and His name is the highest name by which God is revealed (Philippians 2:9-11; Colossians 1:15). Jesus is the only divine being we will see in heaven; to see Him is to see

God in the only way that God can be seen (John 14:9).

Many trinitarians expect to see three physically separate and distinct personages; this notion is tritheism. Some trinitarians, such as Bernard Ramm, dodge the issue by saying they do not know whether they will see one or three.[14] W. A. Criswell, past president of the Southern Baptist Convention, gave the only explanation consistent with biblical monotheism, describing the deity of Christ in terms identical to the Oneness view:

> We are not going to see three Gods in heaven. . . . There is one great Lord God. We know Him as our Father, we know Him as our Saviour, we know Him as the Holy Spirit in our hearts. There is one God and this is the great God, called in the Old Testament, Jehovah, and, incarnate, called in the New Testament Jesus.[15]

III. Father, Son, and Holy Spirit

Belief in Jesus as the incarnation of the full, undivided Godhead does not negate belief in the Father and the Holy Spirit. The one God existed as Father and Holy Spirit before His incarnation as Jesus Christ, the Son of God, and when Jesus walked on earth as God Himself incarnate the Spirit of God continued to be omnipresent.[16]

The Bible speaks of the Father, Son, and Holy Spirit, but it does not use these titles to indicate three persons "in" the Godhead. God is a personal being, not a generic, abstract substance. Trinitarians sometimes acknowledge this truth by speaking of God as "a person."[17]

The one God is the Father of creation, Father of the only begotten Son, and Father of believers. (See Deuteronomy 32:6; Malachi 2:10; Galatians 4:6; Hebrews 1:5; 12:9.)

The title of "Son" refers to God's incarnation. The man Christ was literally conceived by the Spirit of God and was therefore the Son of God (Matthew 1:18-20; Luke 1:35).

The title of "Holy Spirit" refers to God in activity. It describes God's fundamental nature, for holiness forms the basis of His moral attributes while spirituality forms the basis of His nonmoral attributes. The title is particularly used of works that God can do because He is a Spirit, such as anointing, regenerating, indwelling, and sanctifying humanity. (See Genesis 1:1-2; Acts 1:5-8.)

These three roles are necessary to God's plan of redemption for fallen humanity. In order to save us, God had to provide a sinless Man who could die in our place—the Son. In begetting the Son and in relating to humanity, God is the Father. And in working in our lives to empower and transform us, God is the Holy Spirit.

In sum, the titles of Father, Son, and Holy Spirit describe God's redemptive roles or revelations, but they do not reflect an essential threeness in His nature. Father refers to God in family relationship to humanity; Son refers to God in flesh; and Spirit refers to God in spiritual activity. For example, one man can have three significant relationships or functions—such as administrator, teacher, and counsellor—and yet be one person in every sense. God is not defined by or limited to an essential threeness.

The Bible identifies the Father and the Holy Spirit as one and the same. The title of Holy Spirit simply describes what the Father is, for God is a Spirit (John 4:24). The Holy Spirit is literally the Father of Jesus, since Jesus was conceived by the Holy Spirit (Matthew 1:18,

20). When the Bible speaks of the man Jesus in relationship to God it uses the title of Father, but when it speaks of the action of God in causing the baby Jesus to be conceived it uses the title of Holy Ghost so that there will be no mistake about the supernatural, spiritual nature of this work.

The Bible calls the Holy Spirit the Spirit of Yahweh, the Spirit of God, and the Spirit of the Father. The Spirit is not a separate person from the Father but pertains to, or is the essence of, the Father (Matthew 10:20). The Bible attributes many works of the Father to the Spirit, such as resurrecting Christ and indwelling, comforting, sanctifying, and resurrecting believers.

The title of "Son" sometimes focuses solely on the humanity of Christ, as in "the death of his Son" (Romans 5:10). Sometimes it encompasses both deity and humanity, as in "Hereafter shall ye see the Son of man sitting on the right hand of power, and coming in the clouds of heaven" (Matthew 26:64). It is never used apart from God's incarnation, however; it never refers to deity alone.

The phrases "God the Son" and "eternal Son" are non-biblical; the Bible instead speaks of the "Son of God" and the "only begotten Son." The Son is not eternally begotten by an incomprehensible, ongoing process; rather, the Son was begotten by the miraculous work of the Spirit upon Mary's womb. The Son had a beginning, namely, at the Incarnation (Luke 1:35; Galatians 4:4; Hebrews 1:5). The Son was begotten once, not twice as the Athanasian Creed holds.

One day the redemptive plan for which God manifested Himself in flesh will be complete. God will continue to reveal Himself through the immortal, glorified human body of Christ, but the mediatorial role of the Son will end. Jesus Christ will rule eternally, not as the Son, but as God, Father, Creator, and Lord of all (I Corinthians 15:28).

How does "the Word" in John 1 relate to the Son? While both terms refer to Jesus Christ, "Word" is not equivalent to "Son," for the latter is limited to the Incarnation while the former is not. In the Old Testament, God's Word *(dabar)* was not a distinct person but was God speaking, or God disclosing Himself (Psalm 107:20; Isaiah 55:11). To the Greeks, the Word *(logos)* was not a distinct divine person, but reason as the controlling principle of the universe. The noun *logos* could mean thought (unexpressed word) as well as speech or action (expressed word).

In John 1, the Word is God's self-revelation or self-disclosure. Before the Incarnation, the Word was the unexpressed thought, plan, reason, or mind of God. In the beginning, the Word was with God, not as a distinct person but as God Himself—pertaining to God much as a man's word pertains to him. The Greek word order is emphatic: "The Word was God Himself" (John 1:1, Amplified). In the fullness of time God revealed Himself in flesh (I Timothy 3:16). "The Word was made flesh" in the person of Jesus Christ (John 1:14). The Word was revealed in the Son.

IV. The Humanity of Jesus Christ
The Scriptures proclaim the genuine and complete humanity of Jesus (Romans 1:3; Hebrews 2:14-17; 5:7-8). However we define the essential components of humanity, Christ had them: flesh, body, soul, spirit, mind, will.[18]

Jesus was both Son of God and Son of man. He was

the only begotten Son of God since God's Spirit caused His conception. He was the Son of man (humanity) since He had a human mother.

"Son of" also means "having the nature or character of," as in "sons of thunder," "sons of Belial," and "son of consolation." Jesus had the very character of God as well as that of perfect humanity. "Son of God" draws attention to His deity as well as His humanity, for no one can be like God in every way, be equal with God, or have God's complete character without being the one God Himself (Isaiah 46:9; 48:11; John 5:18). The identification of Jesus as the unique Son of God signifies that He is God in flesh.

Jesus was a perfect human. He was more than a theophany, and He was more than God animating a human body. He was actually God incarnate—God dwelling and manifesting Himself in true humanity, with everything humanity includes. If He had anything less than full humanity, the Incarnation would not be real and the Atonement would not be complete.

Christ's true humanity does not mean He had a sinful nature, which was not originally part of the human race. He was subject to all human temptations and infirmities, but He was without sin (Hebrews 4:15). He committed no sin, and sin was not in Him (I Peter 2:22; I John 3:5).

It is necessary to distinguish clearly between the deity and the humanity of Christ. While Jesus was both God and man at the same time, sometimes He spoke or acted from the human viewpoint and sometimes from the divine viewpoint. In the words of Henry Thiessen, "Sometimes he would act from his human self-consciousness, at other times from his divine, but the two were never in conflict."[19] We cannot adequately compare our existence or experience to His. What would seem strange or impossible if applied to a mere human becomes understandable when viewed in the context of One who was fully God and fully man at the same time.

For example, as a man He slept one moment, yet as God He miraculously calmed the storm the next moment. On the cross He spoke from human frailty when He said, "I thirst." Yet when Jesus said, "Thy sins be forgiven thee," He spoke with His power and authority as God. When the Bible says Christ died, it refers to human death only, for deity cannot die. When it says Christ dwells in the hearts of believers, it refers to His divine Spirit.

Only as a man could Jesus be born, grow, be tempted by the devil, hunger, thirst, become weary, sleep, pray, be beaten, die, not know all things, not have all power, be inferior to God, and be a servant. Only as God could He exist from eternity, be unchanging, cast out demons by His own authority, be the bread of life, give living water, give spiritual rest, calm the storm, answer prayer, heal the sick, raise His body from death, forgive sin, know all things, have all power, be identified as God, and be King of kings. In an ordinary person, these two contrasting lists would be mutually exclusive, yet the Scriptures attribute both to Jesus, revealing His dual nature.

This distinction between deity and humanity explains the biblical distinction between Father and Son. Any attempt to make them two persons runs into either the Scylla of tritheism or the Charybdis of subordinationism. And many popular trinitarian arguments fail even when examined in light of trinitarian Christology. For example, many trinitarians say the two wills of the Father and Son require two divine persons, yet the sixth trinitarian ecumenical council (Constantinople, A.D. 680) acknowledged that Christ had two wills but was only one person.

Although we must distinguish between Christ's deity and humanity, it is impossible to separate the two in Him. His human spirit and His divine Spirit were inseparable; in fact, it may be more proper to speak of the human aspect and the divine aspect of His one Spirit. While two distinct wills were present in Christ—divine and human—the two never acted in conflict. While Christ lived as a man, He was always conscious of His deity.

Several passages of Scripture describe the inseparable union in Jesus Christ. (See John 1:1, 14; 10:30, 38; 14:10-11.) It seems clear that God has made the union eternal, that Christ's basic nature will not change (Hebrews 13:8), that He will never cease to be God and man united.

In John 10:30, Jesus did not say, "I am the Father," but "I and my Father are one." He thereby stressed not only His identity as the Father but also the union of deity and humanity in Himself. He was more than the invisible Father—He was the Father in the Son, the Deity in flesh. He did not say, "My Father and I agree as one," as if He and the Father were two distinct persons united in purpose only. Rather He expressed that the Father had united with humanity to form one being—Jesus Christ, the Godhead incarnate.

In John 14:10-11, Christ's statement "The Father [is] in me" is a powerful Oneness text, but He also said, "I am in the Father." In other words, His humanity was elevated in a total union with deity. He did not lose the distinctiveness of His humanity, but His humanity was joined with deity in a way not true of any other man. His words speak of a complete and permanent union of essence.

Even the cross did not destroy this union (Hebrews 9:14). The Father remained with and in Christ to the end (John 16:32). When Jesus cried out, "My God, my God, why hast thou forsaken me?" (Matthew 27:46), He was not stripped of deity. He simply expressed genuine human emotion as He experienced the feeling of the separation from God that will occur with unrepentant sinners at the last judgment. The Spirit of God still dwelt in Christ but did not protect His humanity from the full brunt of the human suffering.

Death separated the divine Spirit from the human body, but Christ's humanity was more than a body. Even while His body lay in the grave, both humanity and deity remained united in His Spirit. At the resurrection Christ's humanity was glorified, and at the ascension His humanity was exalted. While He is still human, He no longer submits to human limitations and frailties; He is glorified eternally.

While on earth Jesus was fully God, not merely an anointed man. At the same time, He was fully man, not just an appearance of man. He possessed the unlimited power, authority, and character of God. He was God by nature, by right, by identity; He was not merely deified by an anointing or indwelling. Unlike the case of a Spirit-filled person, the humanity of Jesus was inextricably joined with all the fullness of God's Spirit.

Only thus can we describe and distinguish the humanity and deity in Jesus; while He sometimes acted and spoke from one role or the other, the two were not actually separated in Him. We can make only a distinction and not a separation in the humanity and deity that united perfectly in Him.

It divides Christ too much to say He had two personalities; He had a unified personality. At all times His humanity was fully integrated with His deity as much as possible given human limitations. The divine personality permeated and colored every aspect of the humanity. Perhaps we can say that Jesus possessed the complete essence of humanity with His personality seated in His deity.

Ultimately, human explanations of the Incarnation are inadequate. The mystery of godliness is not how God could be both one and three—He is simply one—but how God became a man (I Timothy 3:16). Trinitarians face the same puzzles in understanding the Incarnation as Oneness believers do, but trinitarians are confronted with other complications. Both seek to explain the relationship of deity and humanity in Christ, but trinitarians must also explain the interrelationships of three divine persons, and in addition they must deal with two sons—a human son who was born and died and an eternal son who cannot be born or die.

V. The Name of God

Both testaments emphasize the doctrine of God's name. In biblical thought, an individual's name is an extension of his personality, and the name of God represents His presence, character, power, and authority (Exodus 6:3; 9:16; 23:21; I Kings 8:27-29). In the Old Testament, Yahweh was the sacred, redemptive name of God and the unique name by which He distinguished Himself from false gods (Exodus 6:3-8; Isaiah 42:8). The Old Testament also uses a number of compound names for God that reveal aspects of His character.

In the New Testament, God accompanied the revelation of Himself in flesh with a new name. That name is Jesus, which includes and supersedes Yahweh and all the compound names, since it literally means "Yahweh-Savior" or "Yahweh is salvation." This name expresses that God came to dwell with us and become our Savior (Matthew 1:21, 23). Although others have borne the name Jesus, the Lord Jesus Christ is the only one who actually personifies that name.

Jesus is the redemptive name of God in the New Testament. It is the name of supreme power and authority, the only saving name, the name given for remission of sins, and the highest name ever revealed (John 14:14; Acts 4:12; 10:43; Philippians 2:9-10). When there is an occasion to invoke God's name, Christians should use the spoken name Jesus as an expression of faith in Him and in obedience to His Word (Colossians 3:17).

The early church prayed, preached, taught, healed the sick, performed miracles, cast out unclean spirits, and baptized in the name of Jesus. They refused to remain silent about His name, and they rejoiced when they were counted worthy to suffer for His name.

The name of Jesus is not a magical formula; calling on that name is effective only by faith in Jesus and a relationship with Him (Acts 3:16; 19:13-17).

The Father is revealed to us in the name of Jesus, the Son was given the name of Jesus at birth, and the Holy Spirit comes to us in the name of Jesus (Matthew 1:21; John 5:43; 14:26; 17:6). Thus "the name [singular] of the Father, and of the Son, and of the Holy Ghost" (Matthew 28:19) is Jesus (Luke 24:47). The apostolic church correctly fulfilled Christ's instructions by baptizing all converts in the name of Jesus (Acts 2:38; 8:16; 10:48; 19:5; 22:16).[20]

VI. Explanations of New Testament Passages

Let us analyze a few New Testament passages that trinitarians often use in an attempt to refute Oneness.[21]

• The baptism of Christ did not introduce to the devout Jewish onlookers a radical, innovative doctrine of plurality in the Godhead, but it signified the authoritative anointing of Jesus as the Messiah. The dove was a sign for John, and the voice was a sign for the people. A correct understanding of God's omnipresence and omnipotence dispels any notion that the heavenly voice and dove require distinct persons.

• Plural titles for God identify various attributes, roles, or relationships. For example, II Corinthians 13:14 describes three aspects or works of God—grace, love, and communion—and links them with names or titles that correspond most directly to them—Lord Jesus Christ, God, and Holy Ghost. Likewise, I Peter 1:2 mentions the foreknowledge of God the Father, the sanctification of the Spirit, and the blood of Jesus.

• Plural references to God and Jesus Christ in the New Testament emphasize that we must not only acknowledge the one true God of the Old Testament—the Father and Creator—but we must also acknowledge His revelation in flesh, as Jesus Christ. Salvation does not come to us simply because God is Spirit, but specifically through the atoning death of the man Jesus. Thus to be saved we must know "the only true God" and Jesus Christ, whom He sent (John 17:3).

This concept also explains the typical greeting in Paul's epistles: "Grace to you and peace from God our Father, and the Lord Jesus Christ" (Romans 1:7). If the trinity were in view, we would expect mention of the Spirit.

Likewise, I Timothy 2:5 says there is "one God, and one mediator between God and men, the man Christ Jesus." If there were a second divine person coequal to the first, he could not be the mediator, for he would need someone to mediate between him and sinful humanity just as much as the first person would. The sinless man Christ Jesus who became the sacrifice for sin is the mediator.

• Plural references to Father and Son in the Gospels show the true humanity of Jesus, for the Son is the man in whom God dwelt. Jesus is both Father and Son, but the two terms are not equivalent. We do not say the Father *is* the Son, but the Father is *in* the Son. For example, the Father (the Spirit) did not die, but the Son (the humanity) died.

• The prayers of Christ demonstrate the struggle and submission of the human will. Jesus prayed as a true human, not as a second divine person, for by definition God does not need to pray. As Stagg has explained:

The prayers of Jesus belong to the mystery of incarnation, not to a threefold division in God. Jesus Christ was truly human as well as divine, and out of his humanity he did pray. This is not to be understood as one God praying to another God, or one part of God praying to another part of God. It is to be understood as the prayers which came from an authentic human life, one in which God was uniquely present.[22]

• Jesus frequently stated that the Son was inferior to the Father in power, authority, and knowledge. In these instances, He spoke of His humanity. If these examples are used to demonstrate a plurality of persons, they would establish the subordination of one person to the other, contrary to the trinitarian doctrine of coequality.

• Other descriptions of communion and love between Father and Son show the union of deity and humanity in Christ. If used to demonstrate a distinction of persons, they would establish distinct centers of consciousness in the Godhead, which is in effect polytheism.

• The description of the Spirit as "another Comforter" in John 14:16-18 indicates a difference of form or relationship, that is, Christ in Spirit rather than flesh.

• John 17 speaks of Christ's glory with the Father before the world began. This glory related to Christ's upcoming crucifixion, resurrection, and ascension, which was in the plan of God before creation (I Peter 1:19-20). As a man, Christ prayed for the Father to fulfill the plan. He was not speaking of His glory as God, for He always had it and did not need for anyone to give it back to Him. Moreover, later in the chapter He spoke of giving this glory to His disciples, but God never shares divine glory.

• John 17 also speaks of the unity of the man Christ with the Father. As a man Christ was one with God in mind, purpose, and will, and we can be one with God in this sense. Other passages, however, teach that Christ is one with God in a sense that we cannot be, in that He is God Himself.

• "The God and Father of our Lord Jesus Christ" denotes a covenant relationship, much as "the God of Abraham." It reminds us that the promises Christ won as a sinless man are available from God to those who have faith in Christ.

• The humiliation of Christ described in Philippians 2:6-8 does not mean Christ emptied Himself of attributes of deity such as omnipresence, omniscience, and omnipotence, for then Christ would be merely a demigod. The Spirit of God retained all attributes of deity while He manifested all of His character in flesh. This passage only refers to the limitations Christ imposed on Himself relative to His human life. In His life and ministry Christ voluntarily surrendered glory, dignity, and divine prerogatives. He was in very nature God, but He was also a man and He lived as a servant. The person who was the union of deity and humanity was equal to God and proceeded from God, but lived humbly and was obedient unto death.

• God made the worlds (literally, "ages") by the Son (Hebrews 1:2). Certainly, the Spirit of God who later dwelt in the Son was the Creator. Moreover, God based the entire work of creation upon the future manifestation of the Son; He created with the Son in view. God foreknew that humans would sin, but He also foreknew that through the Son they could be saved and could fulfill His original purpose in creation. Though God did not pick up the humanity until the fullness of time, He acted upon it from all eternity. The Lamb was "foreordained before the foundation of the world, but was manifest in these last times" (I Peter 1:19-20).

•Jesus is at the right hand of God. This phrase does not denote a physical positioning of two beings with two

bodies, for God is a Spirit and does not have a physical
body outside of Jesus Christ. This view would be indistin-
guishable from belief in two gods. Rather, the phrase is an
idiomatic expression from the Old Testament denoting
that Christ possesses all the power, authority, glory, and
preeminence of God (Exodus 15:6; Matthew 26:64-65;
Acts 2:34). It also describes His present mediatorial role
(Romans 8:34; Hebrews 8:1). Stephen did not see two
divine persons; He saw the exalted Christ radiating all the
glory of God, and He called upon God by saying, "Lord
Jesus, receive my spirit" (Acts 7:55-60).

VII. Conclusion
We can identify four major themes in the biblical
description of the Incarnation: (1) the absolute and complete deity of Jesus Christ; (2) the perfect, sinless humanity of Jesus Christ; (3) the clear distinction between the
humanity and the deity of Jesus Christ; and yet (4) the
inseparable union of deity and humanity in Jesus Christ.

Jesus is the fullness of God dwelling in perfect
humanity and manifesting Himself as a perfect human
being. He is not a mere man, a demigod, a second person
"in" the Godhead, a divine person temporarily stripped of
some divine attributes, the transmutation of God into
flesh, the manifestation of a portion of God, the anima-
tion of a human body by God, God manifesting Himself in
an incomplete humanity, or God temporarily dwelling in a
separate human person. Jesus Christ is the incarnation—
embodiment, human personification—of the one God.

Acknowledging both the deity and humanity of Jesus
Christ is necessary to salvation (John 8:24; I John 4:3),
but an intellectual comprehension of the Oneness doc-

trine is not. People are born again as they repent, believe on Christ, and obey His gospel, thereby relying on His identity as both God and man, even though their understanding of the Godhead may be limited, incomplete, or not well integrated.

In contrast to trinitarianism, Oneness asserts the following: (1) God is indivisibly one in number with no distinction of persons. (2) God's oneness is no mystery. (3) Jesus is the absolute fullness of God in flesh; He is Elohim, Yahweh, Father, Word, and Holy Spirit. (4) The Son of God was begotten after the flesh and did not exist from eternity past—the term refers to God's incarnation as Christ. (5) The Word is not a distinct person, but the mind, thought, plan, and revelation of God. (6) Jesus is the revealed name of God in the New Testament, and it represents salvation, power, and authority from God. (7) We should administer water baptism by orally invoking the name of Jesus. (8) We receive the abiding presence of Christ into our lives when we are filled with the Holy Spirit. (9) We will see one divine person in heaven: Jesus Christ.

The Oneness doctrine upholds biblical Christianity in at least three ways: (1) It restores biblical terms and patterns of thought on the subject of the Godhead, clearly establishing New Testament Christianity as the spiritual heir to Old Testament Judaism; (2) It affirms the absolute deity of Jesus Christ, revealing His true identity; and (3) It places biblical emphasis on the name of Jesus, making the power of His name available to the believer.

The Oneness doctrine emphasizes that our Creator is also our Savior. The God against whom we sinned is the One who forgives us. (Indeed, no one else has the authority to forgive us except the One whose law we violated.) God loved us so much that He came in flesh to save us. He gave of Himself; He did not send someone else (II Corinthians 5:19).

Moreover, our Creator-Savior is also the indwelling Spirit who is ever present to help us. God first told us how to live and then came to live among us. As a man, He showed us how to live and purchased eternal life for us by laying down His human life. Now He abides within us and enables us to live according to His will.

Jesus Christ is the one God incarnate, and in Him we have everything we need—healing, deliverance, victory, and salvation (Colossians 2:9-10). By recognizing the almighty God in Jesus Christ we restore correct biblical belief and experience apostolic power.

2

The Word Became Flesh

In the beginning was the Word, and the Word was with God, and the Word was God. . . . And the Word became flesh, and dwelt among us, and we beheld His glory, the glory as of the only begotten of the Father, full of grace and truth (John 1:1, 14, NKJV)

The message of the Bible is that our Creator became our Savior. Jesus Christ is "God with us" who came to "save his people from their sins" (Matthew 1:21, 23). "God was in Christ, reconciling the world unto himself" (II Corinthians 5:19).

The Gospel of John expresses this beautiful truth in unique fashion, speaking of Jesus as "the Word" made flesh. Unfortunately, some have interpreted its statements to mean that Jesus is a second divine person. But what does the Bible really say?

In the Old Testament, God's Word (*dabar* in Hebrew) was not a distinct person but was God speaking, acting, or disclosing Himself. "He sent his word, and healed them, and delivered them from their destructions" (Psalm 107:20). "So shall my word be that goeth forth out of my mouth: it shall not return unto me void, but it shall accomplish that which I please, and it shall prosper in the thing whereto I sent it" (Isaiah 55:11). God's Word was the expression of God's mind, thought, and purpose, which was God Himself.

There was no hint of compromising the absolute oneness of God. (See Deuteronomy 6:4.) The Hebrews knew that God stands alone and by Himself: no one is beside Him, no one is like Him, no one is His equal, and no one helped Him create the world. (See Isaiah 44:6, 8, 24; 45:5-6; 46:5, 9.) He is the only Creator and only Savior (Isaiah 37:16; 43:11).

In New Testament times, the Word *(Logos)* was a popular philosophical concept. In the prevailing Greek culture of the eastern Roman Empire, the Word meant reason as the controlling principle of the universe. In Greek the noun *logos* could mean thought (unexpressed word) as well as speech or action (expressed word). As an example, it could refer to a play as conceived in the mind of the playwright, as written in the script, or even as acted upon the stage.

For the apostle John, a Jew trained in the Old Testament, the Hebrew background of "the Word" was undoubtedly the most significant. At the same time, he surely knew how his pagan contemporaries used the term. Under divine inspiration he used it in a unique way to point both Jews and Gentiles to Jesus Christ.

John did not contradict the Jewish concept of the absolute oneness of God with no distinction of persons. In fact, he recorded Christ's statement to a Samaritan woman that the Jews had the correct concept of God: "Ye worship ye know not what: we know what we worship: for salvation is of the Jews" (John 4:22). But John sought to reveal the identity of Jesus as the one God incarnate. He presented as true the words of Thomas, an enlightened Jew, who confessed Jesus as "my Lord and my God." (See John 20:28-31.)

John used the Greek term for "the Word" as a point of reference for his readers, but unlike the Greek philosophers, he made clear that the Word was eternal, was actually God, and was revealed in the human person of Jesus Christ. The Word is our Creator, our source of life, the light of the world, and our Savior (John 1:3-13).

By contrast, Philo, a Jewish philosopher of Alexandria in the first century A.D., sought to blend Jewish and Greek thought by speaking of the Word as an impersonal agent of God by which He created the world and relates to it. Similarly, Justin, a philosopher who lived in the mid second century and converted to Christianity, tried to express Christianity in terms of Greek philosophy. He described the Word as a subordinate second person who was begotten by God at a point in time before creation and who became God's agent of creation. Justin's ideas, shared by some other second-century writers called Greek Apologists, influenced the development of the doctrine of the trinity in the third and fourth centuries.

John's usage is clearly incompatible with these ideas. The Word was not begotten at a point in time; rather, "in the beginning was the Word, and the Word was with God." Moreover, the Word was not a subordinate agent, creature, or begotten being; "the Word was God." John's choice of word order in the Greek here is emphatic, signifying, "The Word was God Himself" (Amplified Bible).

A trinitarian explanation of John 1:1 is inadequate and would require a midsentence change of the definition of "God." Is God "the Father" (as I Corinthians 8:6 states)? If so, "the Word was with [the Father], and the Word was [the Father]." Is God "the trinity"? If so, "the Word was with [the trinity], and the Word was [the trinity]." But trinitarians try to have it both ways, saying, "The Word was with God [the Father], and the Word was God [the Son]." Such an interpretation is inconsistent and erroneous.

John 1:1 is actually a strong statement of the deity of Jesus and of the priority of the Incarnation and Atonement in the mind of God. From the beginning God foresaw the need for the Atonement and so planned the Incarnation. (See I Peter 1:19-20; Revelation 13:8.) From the beginning, God's Word—His mind, reason, thought, plan—was with Him. The Greek preposition here is *pros*, which is not the normal word used to mean "with" but a word most frequently translated as "to." The connotation is not of one person sitting beside another, but of God's Word pertaining to Him or being related to Him.

God's Word is not a distinct person any more than a man's word is a different person from him. Rather, God's Word is the sum total of His mind, reason, thought, plan, and expression, which is God Himself, just as a man's mind is the true man himself.

In the fullness of time and exactly according to God's

predetermined plan, God's Word became flesh and dwelt among us. God enacted His plan. He uttered Himself. The eternal Word was expressed in human flesh, in space and time. In short, the Word is God's self-disclosure or God in self-revelation.

It is interesting to compare these conclusions with the comments of the renowned Christological scholar Oscar Cullman on the Word in John 1:1:

> The author's purpose is specifically to nip in the bud the idea of a doctrine of two gods, as if the Logos were a god *apart from* the highest God. The 'Word' which God speaks is not to be separated from God himself; it 'was with God.'. . . Nor is the Logos subordinate to God; he simply belongs to God. He is neither subordinate to God, nor a second being beside God. . . . One cannot say *theos en pros ton logon* (God was with the Word), because the Logos is God himself in so far as God speaks and reveals himself. The Logos is God in his revelation. Thus the third phrase of the prologue can actually proclaim *kai theos en ho logos* (and the Word was God). We ought not to reinterpret this sentence in order to weaken its absoluteness and sharpness. . . .
>
> The evangelist means it literally when he calls the Logos 'God.' This is confirmed also by the conclusion of the Gospel when the believing Thomas says to the risen Jesus, 'My Lord and my God' (John 20:28). With this final decisive 'witness' the evangelist completes a circle and returns to his prologue. . . .
>
> We can say of this Logos, 'He is God'; but at the same time we must also say, 'He is *with* God.' God and

the Logos are not two beings, and yet they are also not simply identical. In contrast to the Logos, God can be conceived (in principle at least) also apart from his revelatory action—although we must not forget that the Bible speaks of God *only* in his revelatory action. . . .

The Logos is the self-revealing, self-giving God— God in action. This action only is the subject of the New Testament. . . . By the very nature of the New Testament Logos one cannot speak of him apart from the action of God.[1]

In Greek, the word for "dwelt" in John 1:14 is *skenoo*, which literally means "tabernacled" or "tented." The eternal Word was robed in true humanity. God's Spirit was not transmuted into flesh; rather, "God was manifest in the flesh" (I Timothy 3:16). Through this incarnation (embodiment, human personification), we have access to divine glory, grace, and truth. The incarnate Word displays God's glory, communicates God's grace of salvation, and declares God's eternal truth.

Trinitarians use the terms "Son" and "Word" as if they were completely interchangeable, but the Bible speaks of the Son only in reference to the Incarnation. Jesus is the Son of God because the Spirit of God miraculously caused His conception in the womb of the virgin Mary (Luke 1:35). The Son was "made of a woman, made under the law" (Galatians 4:4), and therefore begotten on a certain day (Hebrews 1:5). The Son is "the image of the invisible God" (Colossians 1:15). The Bible never speaks of an eternal Son, but of the "only begotten Son" (John 3:16). By contrast, the Word is God in self-revelation without necessary reference to the Incarnation, and therefore is eternal and invisible.

The two terms, then, are closely related but distinct. The Word was made flesh in the person of Jesus Christ, the Son of God. Only at that point did people behold "the glory as of the only begotten of the Father." The Word was revealed in the Son. In other words, the invisible God was made visible in the Son, who, as a man, has the closest possible relationship or companionship with God. "No man hath seen God at any time; the only begotten Son, which is in the bosom of the Father, he hath declared him" (John 1:18).

In I John 1, the apostle John used the same themes of the eternal Word and the begotten Son, identifying "the Word" as the eternal life of the Father. That life was always with the Father, but not as a distinct person any more than a man's life is a different person from him. And that life was manifested to us in the Son. Therefore, we enjoy spiritual life today not only because God our Father created us but specifically because He provided a plan of salvation for us through the Son. "That which was from the beginning, which we have heard, which we have seen with our eyes, which we have looked upon, and our hands have handled, concerning the Word of life—the life was manifested, and we have seen, and bear witness, and declare to you that eternal life which was with the Father and was manifested to us—that which we have seen and heard we declare to you, that you also may have fellowship with us; and truly our fellowship is with the Father and with His Son Jesus Christ" (I John 1:1-3, NKJV).

According to John 1 and I John 1, then, Jesus is the plan of God enacted, the mind of God disclosed, the life of God manifested. In short, Jesus is the one God Himself revealed in flesh for our salvation. He explained, "I am the way, the truth, and the life: no man cometh unto the Father, but by me. If ye had known me, ye should have known my Father also: and from henceforth ye know him, and have seen him" (John 14:6-7). When we see Jesus, we see the Father in the only way the Father can be seen, for the invisible Father dwells in the visible man Jesus (John 14:9-10). When we accept and apply the atoning work of Jesus, the Son of God, then God's eternal Word is revealed to us. We find the way, the truth, and the life, and thereby we are reconciled to the one true God, our Father.

3

The Almighty God As a Humble Servant

Let this mind be in you, which was also in Christ Jesus: who, being in the form of God, thought it not robbery to be equal with God: but made himself of no reputation, and took upon him the form of a servant, and was made in the likeness of men: and being found in fashion as a man, he humbled himself, and became obedient unto death, even the death of the cross. Wherefore God also hath highly exalted him, and given him a name which is above every name: that at the name of Jesus every knee should bow, of things in heaven, and things in earth, and things under the earth; and that every tongue should confess that Jesus Christ is Lord, to the glory of God the Father (Philippians 2:5-11).

The central truth of Scripture is the marvelous revelation that God came in the flesh to be our Savior. Jesus Christ was miraculously conceived by the Holy Spirit and born of the virgin Mary. He was thereby the human Son of God (Luke 1:35) and actually God manifest in the flesh (I Timothy 3:16). He was truly God, and He was also truly man. In order to provide the way of salvation for us, He did not insist upon His privileges as God, but He lived a humble human life, served human needs, and submitted to death on the cross.

The very name of Jesus describes who He is and what He did for us, for it literally means "Jehovah-Savior." Although others have borne that name, Jesus Christ of Nazareth is the only one who truly personifies it. In other words, Jesus is actually the one God of the Old Testament who came in flesh to be our Savior. Thus the name of Jesus fulfills the prophecy of Isaiah that the Son would be called Emmanuel, which means "God with us" (Matthew 1:21-23).

One of the most profound passages relative to the life and ministry of Jesus Christ is Philippians 2:5-11. Unfortunately, it has been greatly misinterpreted by trinitarians. Let us look at it afresh to uncover its truths.

The Mind of Christ Jesus

First of all, it is important to understand the context of this passage, which refers to Christ's human life and earthly ministry. Verse 5 introduces the subject by saying, "Let this mind be in you, which was also in Christ Jesus." The focus is not on the transcendent nature of God, which we humans cannot duplicate, but on the attitude and conduct of the man Christ Jesus, which we can imitate. The passage recognizes Christ's identity as the almighty God incarnate but emphasizes His human role as a lowly servant.

Verse 6 reminds us that Christ is the true God in order to point out that He had every right to live in this world as a conquering king instead of a humble servant. Nevertheless, as verses 7-8 describe, Jesus did not hold on to His divine prerogatives but relinquished them, living a simple life and enduring a humiliating death. He could have displayed His divine glory to the world and demanded luxury, obeisance, and submission, but instead He voluntarily laid aside these prerogatives in order to atone for our sins.

The New International Version (NIV) translates verses 6-8 as follows: "Who, being in very nature God, did not consider equality with God something to be grasped, but made himself nothing, taking the very nature of a servant, being made in human likeness. And being found in appearance as a man he humbled himself and became obedient to death—even death on a cross."

Equality with God

Trinitarians interpret this passage to mean that a second divine person (the eternal Son) existed; he was equal to but distinct from the Father, and he became incarnate. But this view destroys the numerical oneness of God as taught in Scripture (Deuteronomy 6:4; Galatians 3:20).

As we have seen, this passage draws attention not to the eternal nature of God but to the historical person of Jesus Christ. Verse 6 speaks of One who is both God and man and says that by right He was "equal with God." In other words, Jesus, as God incarnate, was fully equal in every way to God before the Incarnation. God incarnate is the same as God preincarnate. In the Incarnation, God did not lose any of His nature or attributes, which makes the servant role of Jesus all the more amazing.

The use of "equal" does not require Jesus to be a second person. If it did, the Bible would have a contradiction, for God has no equal and there is none like Him (Isaiah 46:5, 9). Moreover, if "equal with" indicates a distinct person, then Jesus would not merely be a distinct person from the Father, as trinitarians teach, but a distinct person from God altogether, which they deny; for verse 6 does not say "equal with the Father" but "equal with God." If God is a trinity and if equality implies a personal distinction, then Jesus is equal to the whole trinity yet a distinct person from the trinity.

The proper understanding of "equal with" in this context is "the same as; identical to." Acts 11:17 provides a similar example in which the same Greek word *(isos)* is translated as "the like," meaning "the same." In John 5:18 some Jewish leaders accused Jesus of "making himself equal with God." They were not accusing Jesus of calling Himself a member of a trinity, for such a concept would have been completely foreign to them. As John 10:33 shows, they were accusing Jesus of claiming to be the one God Himself: "Thou, being a man, makest thyself God." They understood His assertion, but they erred in rejecting it.

There may be a further significance in the use of the plural neuter form in the Greek here, as John Miller, a nineteenth-century Presbyterian minister, explained:

> A simple singular masculine might at once be expected. "Thought it not robbery to be an equal Person with God." Instead of that, it is neuter: and instead of the singular, it is plural. . . . He was truly God. But

His humanity was not truly God. And, therefore, there were certain definitions to be made. . . . Hence the beauty of the language, "that there should be equal respects with God" *(to eina isa)*.

This is no . . . fixing of a Second Person. It is the portrait of a man: of a man claiming to be divine; of a man, actually God in the incarnation of the whole of Deity; but a man not ceasing to be man; and therefore, when stating His equality with God, exquisite in His speech, and carefully reserving respects in which He has still humanity.[1]

Being in the Form of God

Philippians 2:5-6 refers to "Christ Jesus," namely to the divine-human person after the Incarnation took place, not to a second divine person before the Incarnation. Some trinitarians say that the word "being" (Greek, *huparchon*) in verse 6 means "originally being, eternally being, preexisting" and thus speaks of an eternal Son before the Incarnation. But the simple meaning of "being" is more appropriate, as all major translations and Greek dictionaries recognize.

As another example, Luke 16:23 uses the same Greek word to describe a rich man in hades as "being in torments." Clearly he was not in torment originally, eternally, or by preexistence. Similarly, I Corinthians 11:7 uses the same Greek word to teach that man "is the image and glory of God"; it does not speak of an eternal, preexistent state or merely of man's original state, but primarily of his present state.

Many commentators say that the word "form" (Greek, *morphe*) refers to a visible form or an external appearance. While *morphe* has this general meaning, the context establishes its precise meaning here. Verse 7 uses *morphe* again ("the form of a servant"), and verse 8 uses a synonym, *schema* ("found in fashion as a man"). Both Lightfoot and Trench assert that here *morphe* connotes what is intrinsic and essential while *schema* connotes what is outward and accidental.

The main subject of the entire passage is the mind of Christ, not His body. "The form of a servant" refers primarily to the nature or character of a servant, not to the physical appearance of a servant. Likewise, since God is an invisible Spirit who does not have a physical body apart from the Incarnation (John 1:18; 4:24), it seems that "the form of God" refers primarily to God's nature or character, not to a visible manifestation, much less a second divine person. Thus, for Jesus to be "in the form of God" means that He was "in very nature God," as the NIV renders. From eternity the Spirit of Jesus was God Himself, and from birth Jesus was the one true God incarnate and not some lesser being.

If "the form of God" means a visible image, then it refers to Jesus after the Incarnation, for it is as the begotten Son, who was "made of a woman," that He is the "image of the invisible God" and the "express image" of God's nature. (See John 1:18; Galatians 4:4; Colossians 1:15; Hebrews 1:3.) At any time in His earthly life Jesus could have appeared in His divine glory, as in the transfiguration and in the postascension appearances to Stephen and John. But instead He veiled His glory and displayed an ordinary human appearance, revealing His true identity only to those who had the eyes of faith.

The Emptying

Philippians 2:7 says that Jesus "made himself of no reputation, and took upon him the form of a servant." Again, this verse does not focus on the act of incarnation, but upon the total human life and ministry of Jesus Christ. Certainly the phrase "was made in the likeness of men" has the act of incarnation in view, but the phrase "being found in fashion as a man" includes the whole scope of His life. Moreover, verse 8 shows that the culminating act in this process was not the Incarnation but the Crucifixion: "he humbled himself, and became obedient unto death, even the death of the cross."

The Greek word translated as "made of no reputation" is *kenoo*, which has the general meaning of "to make empty." Consequently, many trinitarians say that their second divine person surrendered the attributes of omnipresence, omnipotence, and omniscience in the Incarnation, but this view would mean Jesus was merely a demigod on earth. How could Jesus have lacked divine attributes and still have been God? How could God divest Himself of His essential nature?

The Scriptures reveal that in His Spirit Jesus was everywhere present, knew all things, and had all divine power (Matthew 18:20; 28:18; Mark 2:5-12; John 1:48; 3:13). The King James Version and the New International Version convey the correct meaning here: Jesus did not surrender His attributes but His privileges. As Bauer, Arndt, Gingrich, and Danker translate, "He emptied himself, divested himself of his privileges."[2]

Isaiah 53:12 shows that the supreme act of "emptying" occurred at Christ's death: "He hath poured out his soul unto death: and he was numbered with the transgressors; and he bare the sin of many, and made intercession for the transgressors." As a man, Christ was completely submissive to the indwelling Spirit of God. He was obedient to God's plan even to the point of death.

The Exaltation

As the result of Christ's humble, obedient life and sacrificial death, God has highly exalted Him and given Him the name above every name (Philippians 2:9). By implication, if we adopt the same humble, obedient attitude, we can also expect to be exalted (although not in the same measure). (See Matthew 23:12; James 4:10; I Peter 5:6.)

The emphasis here is first on Christ's humanity, for only as a man could Christ be exalted. As to His deity, Jesus always was the Lord, but by virtue of His life, death, resurrection, and ascension He conquered sin, death, hell, and the devil in the flesh. (See Acts 2:32-36; Colossians 2:15; Hebrews 2:14; Revelation 1:18). He thus openly declared His lordship and earned the right to be called Lord as to His glorified humanity. He is not only the King of eternity but also the human Messiah and Savior.

If this passage spoke of one divine person exalting another, the first person would actually have to be greater than—not equal with—the second person in order to exalt him. And if the second person were preexistent and coequal, why would he need to be exalted? If he ever lost his exalted status, how was he still deity?

Philippians 2:9-11 again affirms that Jesus is truly God and not merely a man. The indwelling Spirit of God resurrected, glorified, and exalted the humanity. As a result, one day all creation will meet God in the person of Jesus Christ and acknowledge that Jesus Christ is the

Lord of the universe. In doing so, they will glorify the Father, for the Father has chosen the Incarnation and the name of Jesus as the means of revealing Himself to the world.

The creation will not confess Jesus as a second divine person, but as the one true God of the Old Testament revealed in flesh. Philippians 2:9-11 is actually the fulfillment of Isaiah 45:23, in which Jehovah ("the LORD") declared, "Unto me every knee shall bow, every tongue shall swear." All will confess Jesus as the incarnation of Jehovah, who is the Father (Isaiah 63:16).

Jesus, the Supreme Name

Philippians 2:9-11 shows that Jesus is the supreme name by which the one God has revealed Himself to the world. Most trinitarian scholars say that the supreme name described in verse 9 is Lord. In other words, God has given the man Jesus the supreme title of Lord. It is true that throughout His life Jesus was known as Jesus but was openly and miraculously declared to be Lord by His resurrection and ascension. Nevertheless, this observation does not detract from the supremacy of Jesus as the personal name of God incarnate, for the added title of Lord serves to magnify the name of Jesus and underscore its true meaning.

As an analogy, the highest political office and title in the United States is that of president. George Washington was the president and thus had the highest title; nevertheless, his unique name—the name that embodied his legal identity, power, and authority—was still George Washington. He could not merely sign documents as "Mr. President"; he had to sign them as "George Washington" in order for his signature to be effective.

Likewise, verse 10 says it is specifically at the name of Jesus that every knee will bow. Philippians 2:10-11 does not merely say that everyone will acknowledge the existence of a supreme Lord, for many unsaved people already do that; the significance of these verses is that everyone will specifically acknowledge that Jesus is the one Lord. As Bauer, Arndt, Gingrich, and Danker translate, "when the name of Jesus is mentioned" every knee will bow and every tongue will confess that Jesus Christ is Lord.

Today some people consider Jesus to be a mythical figure or perhaps an obscure Jew who lived about two thousand years ago. Others look favorably upon Him but consider Him merely a martyr, prophet, teacher, demigod, or second divine person. In the last day, however, the humble servant will reveal Himself for who He really is: the almighty God!

4

Who Is the Creator?

In the context of the Bible, which teaches absolute monotheism, identifying the Creator would appear to be simple; namely, the one God is the Creator. Nevertheless, the idea of a multiperson God has evolved in Christendom, leading many people to speak of creation as a cooperative work of several divine persons. Some have even pictured one person called the Father creating the world through an agent or intermediary called the Son. But what does the Bible say?

One Creator

The Bible unequivocally proclaims that there is one Creator and that He is Jehovah (the LORD). The following passages from the Old Testament clearly reveal that one solitary Being created the universe without assistance from anyone else.

• "O LORD of hosts, God of Israel, that dwellest between the cherubims, thou art the God, even thou alone, of all the kingdoms of the earth: thou hast made heaven and earth" (Isaiah 37:16).

• "I am the LORD that maketh all things; that stretcheth forth the heavens alone; that spreadeth abroad the earth by myself" (Isaiah 44:24).

• "For thus saith the LORD that created the heavens . . . I am the LORD: and there is none else" (Isaiah 45:18).

• "Have we not all one father? hath not one God created us?" (Malachi 2:10).

No stronger language could have been used to establish the Creator's absolute numerical oneness than the terms used in these passages, such as "alone," "by myself," and "none else."

"Let Us Make Man"

Despite these unambiguous statements, some suppose from the plural pronouns in Genesis 1:26 that a committee of three divine persons performed the work of creation. Genesis 1:26 reads, "And God said, Let us make man in our image, after our likeness."

Whatever the plural pronouns in this verse signify, they could not contradict the previously examined biblical statements of the Creator's singleness. In fact, the next verse uses a singular pronoun to describe what actually happened: "So God created man in his own image" (Genesis 1:27).

When we look at Adam—the image creature God made in fulfillment of Genesis 1:26—we find that he was one person. Although we may identify various components of a man—such as body, soul, spirit, will, mind—Adam was one being in every sense. As such, he was the image of the one God who created him.

Genesis 1:26 is not a trinitarian proof text. First, if the verse refers to multiple divine persons, it does not identify them specifically as a trinity; many persons or gods could be involved. Second, if God is defined as a trinity, then the words "God said" would indicate that the whole trinity was talking to some other being, which opens the possibility of other deities. If, on the other hand, only one member of the trinity was talking, then why was he not identified by his proper name? If he can be distinguished from the other divine persons by the title "God," then he would appear to be more divine than they, in contradiction to the trinitarian doctrine of coequality. Third, if an eternal or preexistent Son was being addressed, then his mother must have existed at that time also, for the Son was "made of a woman, made under the law" (Galatians 4:4).

If the plural pronouns do not refer to a trinity, then what do they signify? The simplest explanation is that God was communing within Himself. Ephesians 1:11 informs us that God "worketh all things after the counsel of his own will." If a finite human being can make plans with himself by saying, "Let's see" ("Let us see"), and if the rich fool could address his own soul (Luke 12:19), then it is not unreasonable to suppose that the infinite, omniscient God could counsel with Himself.

Jews have traditionally taught that God addressed the angels, not that angels assisted in creation but that God courteously informed them of His plans and created humanity in the spiritual, intellectual, and moral likeness of Himself and the angels. The angels were present at creation (Job 38:4-7), and God does consult with them on occasion, not to obtain guidance but to include them in His plans (I Kings 22:19-22). In three other scriptural passages God spoke in the first person plural, and their contexts make it plausible that He addressed angels (Genesis 3:22; 11:7; Isaiah 6:8).

Another possibility is that God used a majestic or literary plural, which humans use on occasion. (See Daniel 2:36; Ezra 4:18; 7:24.)

It could also be that God spoke prophetically to the future Son of God, for redeemed humanity will be molded into the physical and spiritual likeness of Christ. (See Romans 5:14; 8:29; II Corinthians 3:18; Philippians 3:21.) As we shall see, some New Testament passages convey this thought of creation with the Son in view.

Creation by Jesus Christ
The New Testament reveals that Jesus Christ is the one God of the Old Testament—Jehovah—manifested in the flesh (John 8:58; 20:28; Colossians 2:9; I Timothy 3:16). Thus, as the following passages declare, Jesus is the Creator.

• "All things were made by him; and without him was not any thing made that was made" (John 1:3).

• "By him were all things created, that are in heaven, and that are in earth, visible and invisible, whether they be thrones, or dominions, or principalities, or powers: all things were created by him and for him" (Colossians 1:16).

• "Thou, Lord, in the beginning hast laid the foundation of the earth; and the heavens are the works of thine hands" (Hebrews 1:10).

Some of the passages that speak of Jesus as the Creator also refer to Him as the Son. (See Colossians 1:13; Hebrews 1:8.) Consequently, trinitarians maintain that an eternal Son co-created the world alongside a distinct person called the Father. But these passages can be understood as simply stating that the One who later became the Son created the world. For example, when we say, "President Lincoln was born in Kentucky," we do not mean that he was president at that time. Rather, the one who later became president was born there.

The title "Son" refers to the humanity conceived in the womb of Mary. (See Luke 1:35; Galatians 4:4; Hebrews 1:5.) As such, the Son did not exist before the Incarnation and did not create the world in the beginning. The Creator is the eternal Spirit of God who later incarnated Himself in the Son and was manifested as Jesus Christ.

Creation with the Son in View

Some passages express a further truth: God created the world with the Son in view, or in dependence upon the future manifestation of Himself in the Son. "God . . . hath in these last days spoken unto us by his Son, . . . by whom also he made the worlds" (Hebrews 1:1-2).

God based all creation on the future Incarnation and Atonement. Though He did not pick up the humanity until the fullness of time, the Incarnation was His plan from the beginning, and He acted upon it from the start. In the plan of God, the Lamb was "slain from the foundation of the world" (Revelation 13:8). The Lamb was "foreordained before the foundation of the world, but was manifest in these last times" (I Peter 1:19-20).

How and why did God depend upon the Incarnation at creation? God created humans in the beginning so that they would love Him, worship Him, have fellowship with Him, give Him glory, and perform His will. (See Isaiah 43:7; Revelation 4:11.) At the same time, God foreknew that they would fall into sin and thereby defeat His purpose for creation. But God, "who calleth those things which be not as though they were" (Romans 4:17), also had in His mind the Incarnation and the plan of salvation through the atoning death of Christ. Even though He knew humanity would sin, He also knew that through the Son of God humanity could be restored and could still fulfill His original purpose. In this sense God created the world through the Son, or by using the Son. In the same way, God justified Old Testament believers on the basis of the future Cross (Romans 3:25).

This explanation fits Hebrews 1. Verse 2 shows that the Son was not eternal but is the revelation of God "in these last days." Verse 3 shows that the Son is not another divine person but rather "the brightness of his [God's] glory, and the express image of his [God's] person." The word "worlds" in verse 2 is from the plural of the Greek word *aion*, which is usually translated "age." This word possibly connotes that God's creative work "by the Son" relates to time, to redemptive history. Thus some translations say that by the Son God created "the ages," "all orders of existence," or "this world of time."

Other verses also show that God created and now sustains all things "by" Jesus Christ in the sense of purpose and plan. "To us there is but one God, the Father, of whom are all things, and we in him; and one Lord Jesus Christ, by whom are all things, and we by him" (I Corinthians 8:6). Ephesians 3:9 says, "God . . . created all things by Jesus Christ," and verse 11 speaks of "the eternal purpose which he purposed in Christ Jesus our Lord."

A study of Greek reinforces this understanding. Colossians 1:16 uses two Greek prepositions to say that all things were created "by" the Son. The first preposition is *en*, literally "in." Colossians 1:16 also uses the preposition *dia*, as does Hebrews 1:2 and I Corinthians 8:6, and it literally means "through." In other words, Christ was not a second person who served as the agent of creation (which would make Him subordinate, and not coequal as trinitarians teach). Rather, we can say that God created all things in Christ and through Christ.

Conclusion

The one God, who is known by various names and titles such as Father, Word, Holy Spirit, and Jehovah, is our Creator. In view of the impending Fall of humanity, God's plan of creation was predicated upon the man Jesus Christ, the Son of God. The church exists and we have spiritual life today not only because of God's initial creative act thousands of years ago but also because of God's redemptive act in Jesus Christ. We are sustained daily by the grace of God bestowed upon us through the Cross, and the living Christ imparts life to us through His indwelling Holy Spirit. The Spirit of Jesus created the human race initially and is yet transforming and molding those who believe in Him, for Jesus is "the author and finisher of our faith" (Hebrews 12:2).

5

Who Is the Holy Spirit?

Since Pentecostals are identified by a strong emphasis on the Holy Spirit, the question arises, What or who is the Holy Spirit? Various groups have defined the Holy Spirit as an abstract principle, an impersonal force, a fluidlike substance, an angel, a subordinate divine being, or the third person in a triune Godhead. But what does the Bible say?

God in Spiritual Activity

God is "the Holy One" (Isaiah 54:5). Only God is holy in Himself; all other holy beings derive their holiness from Him. (See Hebrews 12:10.) Furthermore, God is Spirit (John 4:24), and there is only one Spirit of God (Ephesians 4:4). The title "Holy Spirit" describes the fundamental character of God's nature, for holiness forms the basis of His moral attributes while spirituality forms the basis of His nonmoral attributes. Thus it describes God Himself, the one Holy Spirit.

For example, Peter told Ananias and Sapphira that they had lied "to the Holy Ghost" and then said they had lied "unto God" (Acts 5:3-4). Similarly Paul wrote, "Know ye not that ye are the temple of God, and that the Spirit of God dwelleth in you?" and then, "What? know ye not that your body is the temple of the Holy Ghost?" (I Corinthians 3:16; 6:19).

The Bible calls the Holy Spirit "the Spirit of the LORD [Jehovah]," "my [Jehovah's] spirit," "the Spirit of God" and "his [God's] holy Spirit" (Isaiah 40:13; Joel 2:28; Romans 8:9; I Thessalonians 4:8). These phrases show that the Spirit is not distinct from God but rather pertains to God or is God Himself in spiritual essence. For example, when we speak of the spirit of a man, we do not refer to another person but to the inward nature of the man himself. The man is his spirit and vice versa.

The Bible compares a man and his spirit to God and His Spirit: "For what man knoweth the things of a man, save the spirit of man which is in him? even so the things of God knoweth no man, but the Spirit of God" (I Corinthians 2:11). The former is not two persons, and neither is the latter. We speak of a man's spirit in order to refer to his thoughts, character, or nature, but we do not thereby mean that his spirit is a different person from him or is any less than the total personality. Nor does speaking of God and His Spirit introduce a personal distinction or plurality in Him.

If the Holy Spirit is God Himself, why is this additional

designation needed? What distinction of meaning is intended? The title specifically refers to God in spiritual activity, particularly as He works in ways that only a Spirit can.

The first biblical mention of the Spirit is a good example. Genesis 1:1, speaking in general terms, says, "God created the heaven and the earth." Genesis 1:2, focusing on a specific act of God, says, "And the Spirit of God moved upon the face of the waters." Important spiritual activities of God are regenerating, indwelling, sanctifying, and anointing humanity; thus we usually speak of the Holy Spirit in connection with them. (See Acts 1:5-8.)

The roles of Father, Son, and Holy Spirit are necessary to God's plan of redemption for fallen humanity. In order to save us, God had to provide a sinless Man who could die in our place—the Son. In begetting the Son and in relating to humanity, God is the Father. And in working in our lives to transform and empower us, God is the Holy Spirit.

We should note that the titles "Holy Ghost" and "Holy Spirit" are interchangeable; both are translations of the same Greek phrase. The King James Version uses the former more frequently, but it also uses the latter. (See Luke 11:13; Ephesians 1:13; 4:30.) The latter is usually more understandable to modern English speakers, especially those unfamiliar with the Bible. Frequently, the Bible simply speaks of "the Spirit."

The Spirit of the Father

The Bible identifies the Father and the Holy Spirit as one and the same being. The title of Holy Spirit simply describes what the Father is. There is only one God

(Deuteronomy 6:4). The "only true God" is the Father (John 17:3), and He is Spirit (John 4:24).

The Holy Spirit is the Spirit of the Father, not a different person from the Father. For example, Jesus said that in times of persecution God would give us proper words to say, "for it is not ye that speak, but the Spirit of your Father which speaketh in you" (Matthew 10:20). Jesus spoke of God as our Father in terms of personal relationship, but with reference to supernatural indwelling and anointing Jesus spoke of God as the Holy Spirit.

By definition, the one who begets (causes conception) is the father of the one begotten. The Holy Spirit is literally the Father of Jesus, for Jesus was conceived by the Holy Spirit (Matthew 1:18, 20). If the Father and the Holy Spirit were two persons, then Jesus would have two fathers. When the Bible speaks of the man Christ Jesus in relationship to God it uses the title of Father, but when it speaks of God's action in causing the baby Jesus to be conceived it uses the title of Holy Ghost so that there will be no mistake about the supernatural, spiritual nature of this work.

The Spirit of Jesus Christ

In Jesus Christ dwells all the fullness of the Godhead bodily (Colossians 2:9). Thus the Holy Spirit is literally the Spirit that was in the man Jesus Christ.

All of Christendom confesses that Jesus is Lord, and II Corinthians 3:17 plainly identifies the Lord as the Spirit: "Now the Lord is that Spirit: and where the Spirit of the Lord is, there is liberty." The Bible also describes the Holy Spirit as "the Spirit of Christ," "the Spirit of his [God's] Son," and "the Spirit of Jesus Christ" (Romans 8:9; Galatians 4:6; Philippians 1:19). The way that Christ dwells in our hearts is as the Holy Spirit (Romans 8:9-11; Ephesians 3:14-17).

"Another Comforter"

Trinitarians often point to John 14:16 as evidence that the Holy Spirit is a distinct person: "I will pray the Father, and he shall give you another Comforter, that he may abide with you for ever." But the context reveals that Jesus was speaking of Himself in another form—in Spirit rather than in flesh.

In the next verse He identified the Comforter as someone who already dwelt with the disciples: "Even the Spirit of truth; whom the world cannot receive, because it seeth him not, neither knoweth him: but ye know him; for he dwelleth with you, and shall be in you" (John 14:17). Jesus was the One whom they knew and who dwelt with them. The difference was that the Comforter would soon come in them, in a new relationship of spiritual indwelling rather than physical accompaniment.

And in the following verse Jesus plainly identified Himself as the Comforter: "I will not leave you comfortless: I will come to you" (John 14:18).

Some trinitarians try to avoid this clear designation by saying Jesus was speaking of His physical return, either by the Resurrection or the Second Coming, but both explanations ignore the immediate context. Moreover, the Resurrection would have fulfilled the promise only for forty days, while the Second Coming would not have fulfilled the promise for many centuries, long after the listeners' deaths. Clearly, Jesus spoke of coming and abiding in Spirit, as parallel promises show: "Where two or three are gathered together in my name, there am I in the midst of them" (Matthew 18:20); "I am with you alway, even unto the end of the world" (Matthew 28:20).

"He Shall Not Speak of Himself"

Trinitarians also point to John 16:13 as evidence for an independent personality of the Holy Spirit: "Howbeit when he, the Spirit of truth, is come, he will guide you into all truth: for he shall not speak of himself; but whatsoever he shall hear, that shall he speak: and he will shew you things to come." The Greek text literally says, "He will not speak from Himself," meaning, "He will not speak on His own authority" (NKJV).

A trinitarian explanation of the verse is inadequate, however, for the third person would be in a very subordinate role and possibly would not even be omniscient, contrary to the trinitarian doctrine of coequality. He would not be able to say or know anything except what he received from another person. How then could this third person be God and have the power of God? In fact, this verse says the Spirit does not have independent authority or identity. He does not come under another name but in Jesus' name (John 14:26).

In actuality, Jesus described the baptism of the Holy Spirit and the working of the Spirit in the believer. (See John 16:7.) It seems that He was trying to counter the tendency that sometimes arises among Spirit-filled people to think that they have some kind of supernatural authority in their own right. In other words, people who receive the Holy Spirit do not thereby have authority to establish any doctrine or teaching of their own. Though they may exercise the gifts of prophecy, tongues, and interpretation of tongues, the Spirit within them will not speak as a separate entity residing within them. Rather, the Spirit in them will only speak what is communicated by the mind of God—what is consistent with the Word of God.

To that extent, John 16:13 makes a conceptual (but not personal) distinction between God as Father, Lord, and Omniscient Mind and God in action, operation, or indwelling. The distinction is similar to that in Romans 8:26-27 and I Corinthians 2:10-16. The latter passage says we can know the mind of God by having the Spirit of God in us, for the Spirit of God knows the things of God. But, as we have already seen, the passage clearly does not envisage a personal distinction in the Godhead, for it compares God and His Spirit to a man and his spirit.

Romans 8:26-27 says, "The Spirit itself maketh intercession for us with groanings which cannot be uttered. And he that searcheth the hearts knoweth what is the mind of the Spirit, because he maketh intercession for the saints according to the will of God." In other words, when the Spirit prompts us and speaks through us in intercessory prayer, we can have confidence that our prayers are in God's will. The Spirit of God will certainly make intercession in accordance with the will of God, for the Spirit is God Himself working in our lives. God will act in harmony with Himself as He first motivates our prayers and then hears and answers our prayers.

Conclusion

Pentecostals are sometimes accused of glorifying the Holy Spirit at the expense of Jesus Christ. Oneness Pentecostals are certainly not guilty of this charge, for we recognize that God is one Spirit and that the Holy Spirit is the Spirit of the risen, living Christ. Receiving the Holy Spirit is the way we receive Jesus Christ into our lives.

We do not have two or three divine spirits in our hearts, nor can we identify distinct religious experiences with each of three divine persons. Both the Bible and personal experience tell us that there is one Spirit, the Spirit of our Lord and Savior Jesus Christ. As our Father, God has told us how to live; in the Son God has shown us how to live and provided an atonement for our sins; and as the indwelling Holy Spirit God enables us to live for Him every day.

6

The Son of God

Who is he that overcometh the world, but he that believeth that Jesus is the Son of God? (I John 5:5).

The identity of Jesus as the Son of God is foundational to the Christian faith. On one important occasion Jesus asked His disciples, "Whom say ye that I am?" (Matthew 16:15). Peter replied, "Thou art the Christ, the Son of the living God," whereupon Jesus declared this confession to be a divine revelation and the bedrock of the church (Matthew 16:16-18). Immediately upon his conversion, the apostle Paul preached Christ as "the Son of God" (Acts 9:20).

The apostle John wrote his Gospel so "that ye might believe that Jesus is the Christ, the Son of God; and that believing ye might have life through his name" (John

20:31). He reminded those who had already believed and been born again that in order for God to remain in them, for them to remain in God, and for them to overcome the world, they must continue to realize and acknowledge that Jesus is the Son of God (I John 4:15; 5:5).

What does it mean for Jesus to be the Son of God? According to some people, this title signifies merely that He is a prophet, a powerful man, a king, an angelic being, a demigod, or a junior god. Many others say it means He is a second divine person. But what does the Bible teach?

Conception by the Spirit of God

At its most basic, the phrase "son of" means that the being to whom it applies originates in some way from someone else, whether literally or figuratively. The phrase "son of God" indicates that God is the direct origin and source.

Adam was "the son of God" by creation (Luke 3:38), and so are the angels (Job 1:6; 38:7). Believers are sons of God by adoption into God's spiritual family (Romans 8:14-15).

All Old Testament instances of the phrase "sons of God" or "son of God" conform to this usage. Genesis 6:2, 4 probably refers to godly people, while Job 1:6; 2:1; 38:7; and Daniel 3:25 evidently speak of angels.

As applied to Jesus Christ, the title "Son of God" has both literal and figurative senses. First, no human being was the biological father of Jesus; He was begotten by the spiritual action of God and born of a virgin (Matthew 1:18; 20).

Luke 1:35 provides a biblical definition of the title "Son of God" as it refers to Jesus. "And the angel answered and said unto her [Mary], The Holy Ghost shall come upon thee, and the power of the Highest shall overshadow thee: therefore also that holy thing which shall be born of thee shall be called the Son of God" (Luke 1:35). The word "therefore" announces the reason Jesus is called the Son of God. It is not because He is the incarnation of an eternal second divine person whose name is Son. It is because God caused the conception of the baby Jesus. Jesus is the Son of God for the same reason that any other man is the son of his father—because of the fact of begetting, although in the case of Jesus the begetting was an invisible, supernatural work of God's Spirit.

Begotten at a Certain Time

The Bible never speaks of an "eternal Son," which is a contradiction in terms, but of the "begotten Son." Contrary to trinitarian theory, the Son is not eternal but was formed during the time of the law and in the womb of a woman. "But when the fulness of the time was come, God sent forth his Son, made of a woman, made under the law" (Galatians 4:4).

The Son is not eternally being begotten as orthodox trinitarianism teaches, but the begetting of Jesus occurred at a certain point in human history. "Thou art my Son, this day have I begotten thee" (Psalm 2:7; Hebrews 1:5). The Book of Psalms declares this truth prophetically, while Hebrews explains that the prophecy came to pass in Jesus. Jesus was begotten as a baby in the womb of Mary before His birth in this world (Hebrews 1:5-6), and He was begotten from the dead by His resurrection (Acts 13:33; Revelation 1:5).

The begetting of the Son was still future in the Old

Testament, and therefore all Old Testament references to the Son of God are prophetic. Using II Samuel 7:14 as a type of the Messiah, Hebrews 1:5 depicts God looking to the future: "I will be to him a Father, and he shall be to me a Son." The distinction between Father and Son does not apply to an eternal relationship within the Godhead, but it refers to the relationship of the eternal Spirit of God to the authentic man in whom He dwelt fully. In short, the role of the Son began with the Incarnation.

Trinitarians often cite two Old Testament passages as proof that the Son existed as a second person before the Incarnation. First, Proverbs 30:4 asks, "Who hath ascended up into heaven, or descended? who hath gathered the wind in his fists? who hath bound the waters in a garment? who hath established all the ends of the earth? what is his name, and what is his son's name, if thou canst tell?" The context, however, speaks of human ignorance and error in contrast to divine perfection (Proverbs 30:2-6). The prophet Agur issued a challenge: Do you know anyone who can do what God can? If so, name him, and identify him by telling us who his son is. In other words, no one is God's equal.

Daniel 3:25 records King Nebuchadnezzar's description of the fourth man that appeared in the fire with the three young Hebrew men: "the form of the fourth is like the Son of God." In the original Hebrew text, there is no initial definite article ("the"), and thus the phrase can be rendered "a son of the gods" (NIV). It is unlikely that Nebuchadnezzar knew about the prophecies concerning the Messiah, and it is historically impossible for him to have referred to the doctrine of the trinity. We can be sure of what he meant, for in the same passage he identified the figure he saw as an angel of God (Daniel 3:28). Perhaps this figure was a temporary manifestation of God (a theophany), but if so, nothing indicates that this manifestation had the features of the Son later born of Mary.

God Manifested in Flesh

Jesus was begotten by the Spirit of God and born of Mary, and thus He was both divine and human. Since there is only one God and since the Godhead cannot be divided (Deuteronomy 6:4), it is evident that He was actually God Himself manifested in the flesh (I Timothy 3:16). (See also John 20:28; Titus 2:13.)

This truth becomes apparent in a greater measure as we investigate the figurative aspect of the title "Son of God." In the Bible as well as today, the phrase "son of" is often used to describe someone's nature or character. The expression is apt because by heredity and nurture a son receives attributes and characteristics from his father.

Jesus called James and John "sons of thunder," apparently referring to their violent temper (Mark 3:17), and He described some people as children of the devil because of their evil deeds (John 8:44). The apostles named an early disciple Barnabas, meaning "son of consolation," because he encouraged and comforted others (Acts 4:36).

To say that someone is a son of God, then, connotes that He bears the nature, character, and likeness of God in flesh. When used of ordinary humans or angels, the phrase signifies only an imperfect resemblance, for no one is absolutely like God in every way, and no one is God's equal (Isaiah 46:5, 9).

In the case of Jesus, however, the Bible uses the title "Son of God" in a special way. He is not merely a son of

God, but He is "the only begotten Son of God" (John 3:18). The Greek word *monogenes* in this phrase means "only, unique, one of a kind." Thus the NIV translates, "God's one and only Son."

Jesus is the Son of God in a way that no one else is. His Sonship is different in kind. He does not merely resemble God in some limited ways, but He is equal to God in every way (Philippians 2:6). Indeed, the Son is "the image of the invisible God," "the brightness of his glory, and the express image of his person" (Colossians 1:15; Hebrews 1:2-3).

Jesus exhibited the unlimited power, authority, love, wisdom, holiness, and glory that characterize God alone. He displayed divine power over nature, sin, sickness, the devil, and death. All God's fullness dwells in Him (Colossians 2:9).

As the unique Son of God, Jesus bears the perfect, exact nature, character, and likeness of God in flesh. Since no one can be God's equal and yet be different from God, this statement actually means that Jesus is God Himself manifested in the flesh.

This is in fact how the Jewish religious leaders interpreted Jesus' claim to be the unique Son of God. In John 5:18 they sought to kill him because He said "that God was his Father, making himself equal with God." They did not think He claimed to be the second person of a trinity but to be God Himself. On a later occasion, they explained, "For a good work we stone thee not; but for blasphemy; and because that thou, being a man, makest thyself God" (John 10:33). They correctly perceived that He was claiming deity, but they erred in rejecting His claim. He was not a man trying to make Himself God; He was God who had made Himself man.

The Son Addressed As God

In an attempt to demonstrate that the Son is actually a second divine person, trinitarians sometimes appeal to Hebrews 1:8, which speaks of the Son as God. Verse 9, however, shows that the Son is also a man. The whole passage, then, simply reiterates what we have already seen, namely, that the Son is God manifested in the flesh. "But unto the Son he saith, Thy throne, O God, is for ever and ever: a sceptre of righteousness is the sceptre of thy kingdom. Thou hast loved righteousness, and hated iniquity; therefore God, even thy God, hath anointed thee with the oil of gladness above thy fellows" (Hebrews 1:8-9). Verse 8 speaks of the deity of the Messiah, while verse 9 speaks of His humanity.

This passage does not record a conversation between two divine persons. Rather, it is a quotation of Psalm 45:6-7, a prophetic passage concerning the Messiah to come. To show how God planned for the future, Hebrews 1:8 depicts God as addressing this prophecy to the Son. It is an example of God's calling "those things which be not as though they were" (Romans 4:17). Hebrews 1:5 clearly puts the fulfillment in the future tense: "I will be to him a Father, and he shall be to me a Son."

When we read Psalm 45:6-7, the original prophecy, we do not find a conversation, but simply a statement by the psalmist. Hebrews 1:1 establishes that God spoke by the prophets, and from that perspective Hebrews ascribes the inspired statements of the biblical writers to God Himself. In so doing, it does not imply a discussion between two persons, however. As another example in the same context, Hebrews 1:7 quotes Psalm 104:4 and attributes the statement of the psalmist to God: "And of the angels he saith, Who maketh his angels spirits, and his ministers a flame of fire." This phraseology does not mean that God spoke these words to another divine person, but that He inspired these words for the writer to record.

The Sending of the Son

According to John 3:17 and other verses, God sent His Son into the world. This phrase does not mean that Jesus was a preexistent second person waiting in heaven for another divine person to send Him down to earth. The word "sent" denotes that the man Jesus originated in the supernatural plan and action of God. He was born of a virgin by the power of the Holy Spirit.

Moreover, the word "sent" reveals that the man Jesus was on a divine assignment and commission. In a similar manner, John 1:6 describes John the Baptist as "a man sent from God," even though he clearly did not live in heaven prior to his birth. As a human being, as the Son of God, Jesus was sent out into the world from the womb of Mary, empowered by the Holy Spirit and ordained by the plan of God to be our sacrifice of atonement.

We gain further insight from the Lord's comparison of the sending of the Son to the sending of His disciples. "As thou hast sent me into the world, even so have I also sent them into the world" (John 17:18). "Then said Jesus to them again, Peace be unto you: as my Father hath sent me, even so send I you" (John 20:21). The sending of the Son did not require His preexistence in heaven as a second person any more than the sending of the disciples required their preexistence in heaven.

Nor does this comparison teach us anything about the nature of the Godhead. Some say it requires that the Father and the Son be two persons, just as Jesus and the disciples were distinct persons; but if we press the words to this extreme, then we have tritheism. If God were a trinity of persons as distinct from each other as three men, then we could not escape the conclusion that actually there would be three Gods. The point of identity in the Lord's comparison is simply that both Jesus and His disciples were humans with a divine commission, ordination, and anointing. They both went "into the world" with divine authority, power, and mission.

The Son Who Came Down from Heaven

In a similar vein, Jesus said in John 6:38, "I came down from heaven, not to do mine own will, but the will of him that sent me." Trinitarians maintain that Jesus must have been speaking of Himself as a preexistent second divine person, but the context reveals what He actually meant.

In John 6:31 some Jews cited Scripture to remind Jesus of how God supplied manna to their forefathers in the wilderness: "He gave them bread from heaven." (See Nehemiah 9:15.) In response Jesus contrasted the manna with "the true bread from heaven," and He explained, "The bread of God is he which cometh down from heaven, and giveth life unto the world" (John 6:32-33). In John 6:51, 58 He stated plainly, "I am the living bread which came down from heaven: if any man eat of this bread, he shall live for ever: and the bread that I will give is my flesh, which I will give for the life of the world. . . . This is that bread which came down from heaven: not as your fathers did eat manna, and are dead: he that eateth of this bread shall live for ever."

When the Bible says God supplied manna "from heaven," it does not mean the manna preexisted in a heavenly form, but it means that God, rather than an earthly cause, was the source of the manna. Jesus expressly identified the true bread that came down from heaven as His flesh, which was offered as a sacrifice on the cross. He did not preexist in heaven as a human being of flesh and blood; He was born of Mary as a human.

When Jesus said He came down from heaven, then, He did not mean that He lived in heaven as a distinct human person and then finally came down to earth in His preexistent form. Rather, He meant that God was the author of the Incarnation, the source from which He as a human being came. He was not born by the agency of Joseph or another man, but He was born of a virgin by the power of God's Spirit.

Hebrews 1:6 says God brought "the firstbegotten into the world." Jesus was first begotten miraculously by God in the womb of Mary, and then He was brought forth into the world as a human baby. That the Son came "into the world" does not mean He preexisted as Son in another world first, any more than the disciples did before they went "into the world" (John 17:18).

Since Jesus was God manifested in the flesh, He could say, "I came down from heaven" with reference to His eternal deity. With reference to His human identity, as distinct from the eternal Father, we must not think of a second, preexistent person, for that would require Him to be an eternal human person and would render His birth of Mary an unnecessary charade. Instead we must understand that His flesh "came down from heaven" in that it had a supernatural, divine origin.

The Limitations of the Son

Many passages of Scripture describe the human limitations of the Son. These verses are incompatible with the notion that the Son is a second, coequal divine person, but they support the understanding that the Son is God manifested in the flesh. These passages focus on His humanity alone.

A prime example is Mark 13:32, which says the Father knows something that the Son does not, namely, the time of the Second Coming: "But of that day and that hour knoweth no man, no, not the angels which are in heaven, neither the Son, but the Father." This verse speaks of the Son as a man, not an eternal divine person. Omniscience (having all knowledge) is an integral part of God's nature, so if the Son were an eternal divine person there could never be a time when the Son would not know a certain thing.

Other statements of Christ likewise refer to the Son as a human: "The Son can do nothing of himself" (John 5:19). "I can of mine own self do nothing" (John 5:30). "I came down from heaven, not to do mine own will, but the will of him that sent me" (John 6:38). "My Father is greater than I" (John 14:28).

Trinitarians typically use these and other similar statements in an attempt to prove that the Father and the Son are two distinct divine persons. If the Son is a separate person in these passages, however, then He has no knowledge, He has no power, His will is subordinate to that of the Father, and He is inferior in every way to the

Father. This would destroy the trinitarian doctrines of coequality and consubstantiality (same substance) of their two persons.

When this point is raised, thoughtful trinitarians will acknowledge that these statements refer only to the human limitations of the Son. By this admission, however, in effect they concede that they can only use these passages to prove the Son is distinct from the Father as a human. They cannot use them to prove that the Son is distinct as an eternal divine person.

If they insist on using these passages to establish that the Son is an eternally distinct divine person, then they must also use them to determine what kind of person this Son would be, namely, one who is not omniscient or omnipotent but inferior to the Father in every way. That conclusion would defeat their own doctrine as well as contradict the Bible's many statements of the full deity of Jesus Christ.

The only way to avoid this paradox is to recognize that Jesus Christ, the Son of God, is God manifest in the flesh. As a man, Jesus could speak of His human limitations without detracting from the omnipotence and omniscience of the eternal Spirit of God, who dwelt fully in Him.

The people with whom Jesus conversed knew Him to be a man, and they also knew God to be an invisible Spirit. In order to lead them to an understanding of the Incarnation and to saving faith in Him, Jesus stressed that they should not look at Him merely as a man. His words and actions were not mere human words and actions. He was not acting out of human power, authority, and will. To the contrary, His every word and deed was motivated by the

Spirit of God within Him. He explained, "The words that I speak unto you I speak not of myself: but the Father that dwelleth in me, he doeth the works" (John 14:10). As the human Son of God, He had limitations and was submissive to the will of God, but as God incarnate He had all power and knowledge.

The End of the Son's Reign

The title of "Son" refers to the Incarnation, which occurred for the purpose of our salvation. Since this purpose will one day be completely fulfilled, there is a sense in which the role of the Son will end. Although the Incarnation will never be reversed, the Bible speaks of a time when the reign of the Son will end. In eternity God will continue to reveal Himself through His glorified humanity as Jesus Christ (Revelation 22:3-4), but He will no longer have occasion to act through the capacity of Son.

The passage that enunciates this truth is I Corinthians 15:24-28. For clarity, let us look at it in the NKJV:

> *Then comes the end, when He [Christ] delivers the kingdom to God the Father, when He puts an end to all rule and all authority and power. For He must reign till He has put all enemies under His feet. The last enemy that will be destroyed is death. For "He has put all things under His feet." But when He says "all things are put under Him," it is evident that He who put all things under Him is excepted. Now when all things are made subject to Him, then the Son Himself will also be subject to Him who put all things under Him, that God may be all in all.*

At first glance, this passage may seem problematic for the Oneness position because it distinguishes the Son from the Father. But if the Son is a distinct person here, then contrary to trinitarianism, the Son is clearly subordinate to the Father and distinct from God altogether.

The only explanation consistent with the deity of Christ as expressed throughout Scripture is that here the "Son" refers to the mediatorial role of Jesus. After the last judgment, no one else will need salvation; no one will need Christ's mediatorial work. Jesus is the Son and always will be in the sense of having humanity, but one day He will no longer act in the role for which He was begotten and born as the Son. He will resume His original role as God and Father of all. We will no longer need to put faith in Him as the Son (mediator), but we will worship and adore Him as our Lord and our God.

The foregoing explanation corresponds closely to the conclusions of trinitarian scholars today, as shown by excerpts from two Bible commentaries written by prominent evangelical trinitarian scholars F. F. Bruce and Leon Morris, respectively:

It appears that Paul tends to distinguish th[e] two aspects of the heavenly kingdom by reserving the commoner expression "the kingdom of God" for its future consummation, while designating its present phase by some such term as "the kingdom of Christ." Thus, in I Corinthians 15:24 Christ, after reigning until all things are put under his feet, delivers up the kingdom to God the Father; his mediatorial sovereignty is then merged in the eternal dominion of God.[1]

Paul is not speaking of the essential nature of either Christ or the Father. He is speaking of the work that Christ has accomplished, and will accomplish. He has died for men, and He has risen. He will return again. He will subdue all the enemies of God. The climax of His whole work will come when He renders up the kingdom to Him who is the source of all. In that He became man for the accomplishment of that work, He took upon Him a certain subjection which is necessarily impressed upon that work right up to and including its consummation. The purpose of this *(hina)* is that God may be all in all. This is a strong expression for the complete supremacy that will then so obviously be His.[2]

The language of I Corinthians 15:24-28 is metaphoric and not to be taken as referring to two separate divine persons. Ephesians 5:27 makes clear that Jesus is not going to deliver the kingdom to another divine person: "That he [Christ] might present it to himself a glorious church." Christ loves the church and gave His life for it. It is His bride. He is not going to give His bride, purchased at such great sacrifice, to someone else. No, "God was in Christ, reconciling the world unto himself" (II Corinthians 5:19).

Significance for Us

In summary, Jesus' title of "Son of God" refers to the Incarnation. It is necessarily linked to the elements of humanity and time. The Bible never speaks of "God the Son," as if Sonship were eternally inherent in the Deity, but only of "the Son of God." The Bible describes the Son in terms that could only relate to humanity, not deity existing alone. For example, the Son of God was crucified and the Son died (Romans 5:10; Hebrews 6:6). Only humanity can die. The eternal Spirit of God cannot become unconscious or cease to exist, and neither can a portion of God die.

The Son of God is not merely a human; He is a human in whom the Spirit of God fully dwells. Often, passages that describe the Son have His deity in view, but always in the context of the Incarnation. (See, for example, Mark 2:10; 14:62; Hebrews 1:8-9.)

When we confess that Jesus is the Son of God, then, we confess that He was begotten of a virgin by God's Spirit, that He bears the very nature of God in flesh, and that He is indeed God manifested in the flesh. Moreover, the title is inextricably connected to the purpose for which God came in flesh: to redeem us from sin. Jesus explained, "The Son of man came . . . to give his life a ransom for many" (Matthew 20:28).

Only as a man could Jesus be our kinsman redeemer and our perfect substitute. Only as a man could He shed blood for our sins. Only as a man could He die in our place and thereby pay the penalty for our sins. But only as God does He have power to forgive our sins and be our Savior. Both His true deity and His true humanity are essential to our salvation, and the title "Son of God" encompasses both aspects.

It is no wonder that confessing Jesus as the Son of God is the basis of our salvation and our Christian life. Because Jesus is the Son of God we have a mediator, an advocate, a way of salvation. The Sonship of Jesus allows us to say with the apostle Paul, "The life which I now live in the flesh I live by the faith of the Son of God, who loved me, and gave himself for me" (Galatians 2:20).

Of all people, we should proclaim that Jesus is the Son of God and rejoice in this truth. Let us sing with Bishop G. T. Haywood, an outstanding Oneness Pentecostal pioneer of the early twentieth century:

> O sweet Wonder! O sweet Wonder!
> Jesus the Son of God;
> How I adore Thee! O how I love Thee!
> Jesus the Son of God.

7

The Mediator between God and Men

For there is one God, and one mediator between God and men, the man Christ Jesus (I Timothy 2:5).

The New Testament proclaims that "Christ Jesus came into the world to save sinners" (I Timothy 1:15). This message is of utmost importance to every human being, "for all have sinned, and come short of the glory of God," and "the wages of sin is death" (Romans 3:23; 6:23). Everyone in this world has sinned and needs the Savior.

Humanity's Need and God's Provision

Beginning with Adam and Eve in the Garden of Eden, sin has separated the human race from God, for the holy God cannot have fellowship with sin. Separation from

God means spiritual death, and the ultimate consequence of human sinfulness is eternal separation from God, also called damnation or the second death. In short, God's holiness and justice demand that sin be punished by death.

The human race could devise no way to escape from this dreadful destiny. No person could be his own savior or a savior for others, for each person is himself a sinner under the judgment to die for his own sins. Sinful man could not make himself holy, and the holy God could not become sinful, so there was apparently no common ground on which the two estranged parties could meet.

But in His infinite love, mercy, and wisdom, God designed a plan of salvation that would satisfy the requirements of His holiness and justice and yet provide a means of redemption for sinful humanity. This plan centers on our Lord Jesus Christ, the Son of God, who reunites God and man.

Jesus is the only "mediator between God and man," and as such, He came to "give his life a ransom for all" (I Timothy 2:5-6). He was able to be the unique mediator because He was God manifested in the flesh (I Timothy 3:16; John 1:1, 14). Both His humanity and His deity are essential to His mediatorial work. As a true man, He represents the human race to God; and as the one God incarnate, He reveals the eternal, invisible God to man.

The Man Christ Jesus

Jesus was the only sinless man who ever lived. Thus He was the only man who did not deserve eternal death for sin, and the only person who could be a substitutionary sacrifice for sinful humanity. Just as Adam was the first representative of the human race, leading us into sin by his disobedience to the plan of God, so Jesus serves as the new representative of the human race, leading us into righteousness by His obedience to the plan of God (Romans 5:19).

When we speak of Jesus as the mediator between God and humanity, we must not think of Him as a second God or a second divine person. The Old Testament emphatically proclaims, "Hear, O Israel: The LORD our God is one LORD" (Deuteronomy 6:4). The New Testament does not change this message, for there is no contradiction in the Word of God. Rather, it reiterates the same truth and builds upon it. "There is one God, and one mediator between God and men, the man Christ Jesus" (I Timothy 2:5). The new revelation of the New Testament is not that there is another God or an additional person in the Godhead, which would contradict the faith and doctrine of the Old Testament saints. Rather, the New Testament reveals the same God of the Old Testament in a greater dimension: His coming in flesh to redeem His fallen creation.

Significantly, I Timothy 2:5 does not say the mediator between God and men is "the second person," or "God the Son," or "the eternal Son." It identifies the mediator as "the *man* Christ Jesus" (emphasis added). Christ's role of mediation does not imply a separate divine identity; it simply refers to His genuine, authentic humanity. As God incarnate, Jesus Christ literally unites both deity and humanity in His own person. He Himself is the meeting place of God and man. He becomes the place and means of mediation, not by pointing us to someone else, but by bringing us to Himself, placing us in His body, and filling us with His Spirit.

He is not an agent who leads us into fellowship with another person. "God was in Christ, reconciling the world unto himself" (II Corinthians 5:19). Christ died so "that he might present it to himself [not to someone else] a glorious church, not having spot, or wrinkle, or any such thing" (Ephesians 5:27). When we see and know Jesus, we actually see and know God the Father, because the Father dwells in Jesus (John 14:7-11).

If there were a second divine person, such a person could not be the required mediator between the holy God and sinful humanity. Only a sinless man could be the mediator, the kinsman redeemer, the sacrifice of atonement, the one to shed blood for the remission of sins.

For the sake of argument, let us image that there were two divine persons who were coequal in every way and, in particular, equal in holiness. If a mediator was necessary to bring sinful humanity back into fellowship with the first person, then a mediator would be necessary to bring sinful humanity back into fellowship with the second person. The second person could not serve as the mediator; being just as holy as the first person, he also would need to find or supply someone else as the mediator! In short, it is not a second divine person who is the mediator; it is "the man Christ Jesus" who is the mediator. And this man is specifically the one man in whom the fullness of God dwells by incarnation (Colossians 2:9).

The Mediator As God Incarnate

The mediator had to be a genuine man, but He also had to be God incarnate, for only God can forgive sin. Only Jehovah is the Savior (Isaiah 45:21-22).

Specifically, the mediator had to be the manifestation

of the Father, the Creator, the Lawgiver, the One against whom the human race has sinned from the beginning. If one person wrongs another person, he must confess and apologize to the person he has wronged in order to obtain forgiveness. A third party cannot grant forgiveness and reconciliation. For example, a thief must make restitution to the rightful owner; he cannot give the stolen goods to a third person and secure forgiveness from him. Likewise, as rebellious children we can only go to our heavenly Father to obtain forgiveness and reconciliation. If we look to Jesus as our Savior, we should also acknowledge Him as the revelation of the Father to us. Significantly, Isaiah 63:16 says the LORD (Jehovah) is simultaneously our Father and our Redeemer.

In short, no one else could qualify as the mediator except God Himself coming into this world as a human being. God knew that no one else could be the saving intercessor for the human race, so He provided the means Himself. "He saw that there was no man, and wondered that there was no intercessor: therefore his arm brought salvation" (Isaiah 59:16).

The Basis of Salvation

The only way for us to be saved from eternal death, then, is to turn to Jesus Christ. In a prayer addressed to the Father, Jesus stated the basis of salvation for all humanity: "And this is life eternal, that they might know thee the only true God, and Jesus Christ, whom thou hast sent" (John 17:3).

It should not surprise us that Jesus prayed to the Father; in fact, it should surprise us if He had not prayed. Jesus was a real man in every way; as such, He participated fully in every aspect of human experience, enduring hunger, thirst, weariness, and temptation. As a sinless man who served as the new representative of the human race, He exemplified perfect humanity as God intended it to be, including prayer, obedience, and submission to the will of God. He could do no less and be a righteous man. He could do no less and be a role model for us.

The prayers of Christ do not point to an internal division within the Godhead, but they simply attest to His authentic, complete humanity. If the prayers of Christ proved that He was a second divine person, they would also prove what kind of second person He was—not a coequal person, as trinitarianism teaches, but an inferior person who needed help from the first person. In this case, the second person would not truly be God, for by definition God is all powerful and has no need of assistance. Instead of seeing Jesus as a second, inferior divinity, we must simply recognize that He prayed because He was a man. As Hebrews 5:7 says, He prayed "in the days of His flesh."

In John 17, Jesus prayed as a man to God, addressing the eternal Spirit of God as "Father," even as He instructed us to do in what we call the Lord's Prayer. In John 17:3 He identified the twofold basis of our salvation: knowing the one true God and knowing Jesus Christ. By this spiritual knowledge we can inherit eternal life instead of eternal death.

Like I Timothy 2:5, this verse builds upon the Old Testament truth that there is only one God. Jesus identified the Father as "the only true God" and said that knowing Him is vital to our salvation.

But knowing about the one true God is not enough.

Many Jews of Christ's day worshiped the God of the Old Testament but rejected Jesus, and He said they would die in their sins (John 8:24). Believing in the existence of the Creator and Lawgiver is necessary, but this knowledge alone does not reconcile a person to Him. The only means of reconciliation is through Jesus Christ, for He is the mediator that God has provided. We must specifically know Jesus— the manifestation of the one God—as our Savior. Only when we know Him do we truly know the Father (John 8:19).

We must understand that Jesus was sent from God. As a human being, as the Son of God, Jesus was sent out into the world from the womb of Mary, empowered by the Holy Spirit and ordained by the plan of God to be our sacrifice of atonement. (See chapter 6 for further discussion of the sending of the Son.)

John 17:3 says we need to know "the only true God, and Jesus Christ." This phrase does not refer to two distinct persons in a trinity. If there were a trinity of coequal divine persons, then knowledge of each of them would surely be the necessary basis for salvation, yet there is no mention of a third person. If John 17:3 referred to two persons, then the status of the third person would be compromised. How could knowledge of two persons be required for salvation, yet knowledge of the third coequal person be totally unnecessary?

Moreover, if John 17:3 referred to two persons, then only one of them is God. A comparison of verses 1 and 3 shows that Jesus addressed the "Father" as "the only true God." If Jesus were a different person from the Father, then in this passage He would not be God at all. If "and" in verse 3 distinguishes two persons, then it separates Jesus from God.

That was not the message of either Jesus or John. In John 20:28 Thomas confessed Jesus to be "my Lord and my God." Jesus commended Thomas for his insight and pronounced a blessing on all those who would believe the same truth even without having seen Jesus in the flesh as Thomas had. John recognized the immense significance of this incident. He recorded it with approval and used it as the climax of his Gospel, following it with the thesis statement of the book. Elsewhere, in language reminiscent of John 17:3, John wrote that the Son, Jesus Christ, is "the true God, and eternal life" (I John 5:20).

In sum, our salvation is based upon knowing the true God and specifically knowing Jesus Christ as the manifestation of the true God for the purpose of our salvation. We must act in faith upon this knowledge, applying Christ's death, burial, and resurrection to our lives. In other words, we must believe and obey the gospel of Jesus Christ in order to receive eternal life. "Everlasting destruction from the presence of the Lord" will come upon "them that know not God, and that obey not the gospel of our Lord Jesus Christ" (II Thessalonians 1:8-9).

Our Advocate

In the Old Testament, God saved people on the basis of the future mediatorial work of Christ, but the saints in that era did not have the privilege of seeing His work of redemption fulfilled. They were saved by faith as they obeyed God's plan for their day, but they did not enjoy the knowledge of the Cross, the experience of water baptism in the name of Jesus Christ, the baptism of the Holy Spirit, and the fullness of life in the Spirit. They waited eagerly for the implementation of God's plan but did not live to see it (Hebrews 11:39-40; I Peter 1:10-12).

One of the most patient of Old Testament saints, Job, walked by faith but longed for the opportunity to encounter God more intimately, to have a mediator to bring him into close personal fellowship with God. He lamented, "For he is not a man, as I am, that I should answer him, and we should come together in judgment. Neither is there any daysman [umpire, referee] betwixt us, that might lay his hand upon us both." (Job 9:32-33). In great distress he cried out, "O that one might plead for a man with God, as a man pleadeth for his neighbour!" (Job 16:21).

We have that privilege today. "We have an advocate with the Father, Jesus Christ the righteous: and he is the propitiation [sacrifice of atonement] for our sins" (I John 2:1-2). Jesus Christ is the One who intercedes for us today by His sacrifice on the Cross. Not only have we been redeemed by His atoning sacrifice, but we live daily by the power of His blood; if we sin, we can receive forgiveness today through His blood.

Jesus Christ is our advocate—the One called alongside to help. He is our mediator—the One who brings us into a proper relationship with God. In Him we meet God as our personal friend, helper, and Savior.

8

The Union of the Father and the Son

That they all may be one; as thou, Father, art in me, and I in thee, that they also may be one in us: that the world may believe that thou hast sent me. And the glory which thou gavest me I have given them; that they may be one, even as we are one (John 17:21-22).

An Example for Believers

Shortly before His crucifixion, Jesus prayed to the Father on behalf of His disciples (John 17). As we discussed in chapter 7, the prayers of Christ do not teach us that He was a second divine person but that He was an authentic human being. He prayed "in the days of his flesh" (Hebrews 5:7).

It is from this perspective that we must examine Christ's prayers, including His request in John 17 that the disciples would be one even as He and the Father were one. Trinitarians often attempt to prove from this statement that Jesus and the Father are two persons in the Godhead. They hold that since believers are distinct persons from each other, Jesus must be a different person from the Father.

Unfortunately for trinitarians, this argument proves too much. When carried to its logical end, it does not establish trinitarianism (the doctrine of three persons in one divine substance) but tritheism (the doctrine of three gods). If Jesus meant that He was indeed a distinct person from the Father exactly as believers are distinct from one another, then the three persons of the trinity would be three gods. Moreover, since believers are to be "one in us," arguably they could become members of the Godhead just as Jesus would be.

At this point, trinitarians usually will concede that the oneness of their three persons is different in kind from the oneness among believers. Orthodox trinitarianism teaches that the three persons are one God in a mysterious, incomprehensible way, and not merely one in the sense that three human beings can be united in Christian fellowship.

This concession brings us to the obvious meaning of the passage: Jesus, as a man and referring to His humanity, prayed that believers would enjoy harmony, fellowship, and unity with one another and with God just as He in His humanity did. He Himself manifested this oneness as a sinless, perfect man in relation to God. The oneness of which Jesus spoke in John 17:21-22 is therefore a oneness of mind, purpose, and action, which humans can experience in relation to each other.

Jesus prayed that believers would be one "as thou, Father, art in me, and I in thee" (John 17:21). In this context, He was not speaking of incarnation, for believers cannot be incarnated in one another. He spoke metaphorically of a union of purpose, experience, and love, much as He did in John 14:20: "At that day ye shall know that I am in my Father, and ye in me, and I in you."

To understand John 14:20, let us look first at the phrase "ye in me." Since a believer cannot literally inhabit Christ's body, these words must be understood in the sense of fellowship. This interpretation gives us the key to understanding the parallel phrases "I am in my Father" and "I in you."

"I am in my Father" does not speak of a mysterious "interpenetration" or "circumincession" of two persons of the Godhead that share one divine substance as trinitarians maintain, for then we would have to teach that believers likewise share mysteriously in the divine substance along with Jesus. Such a view would fatally compromise the oneness of God and the uniqueness of Christ. Rather, "I am in my Father" means that Christ's humanity was joined in the closest possible fellowship with God so that as a man He consciously lived, moved, and had His being within the realm of the Spirit.

Likewise the phrase "I in you" speaks of the fellowship that believers experience with Jesus. Other passages teach that Christ dwells in us by His Spirit, but here the primary focus is upon relationship. Just as the man Christ walked in daily fellowship and communion with God, so can we. Since we can enjoy this relationship only by Christ's atoning sacrifice, the Bible speaks of our relationship as specifically with Christ, who is God manifested in flesh for this purpose.

In John 17:22, Christ said, "The glory which thou gavest me I have given them; that they may be one." This statement further shows that in John 17:21-22 He spoke concerning His humanity, not His deity. God is emphatic that He will never share His divine glory (Isaiah 42:8; 48:11). Christ could not give His divine glory to anyone, not even to the apostles. But He did give them the glory of His earthly ministry and the glory that He would receive as a man by dying on the cross to redeem us from our sins.

In short, John 17:21-22 reveals an attribute of the human life of Christ and points to it as an example for us to follow in our relationships. We can be one with each other and with God just as the man Jesus was one with God. It is specifically by His human life that Christ serves as our example (I Peter 2:21). The oneness of God is not the subject of discussion. Rather, John 17:21-22 has Christ's humanity in view in His relationship with the Father, for there is no other way we could be one with each other and with God except according to our own humanity.

The Uniqueness of the Incarnation

Other passages teach that Christ was one with the Father in a way that we cannot be, that is, according to His deity. These passages do not merely teach that Jesus is related to God as one person to another; rather they teach that Jesus is God manifested in the flesh.

For instance, Jesus told some Jews, "I and my Father are one" (John 10:30). He did not say, "I am the Father," because He was not only the invisible Father but also the visible Son. They would not have comprehended such a statement, because they knew the Father to be an invisible Spirit. They thought of the Father as dwelling in heaven, while they saw Jesus as a mere man. In essence Jesus told them, "I, the man who am speaking to you, and the Father, whom you think of as dwelling invisibly in heaven, are not two as you suppose, but I and the Father are one and the same."

The Jews understood Christ's statement as an assertion of deity. They believed in only one God (Deuteronomy 6:4), and they realized that Jesus was claiming identity as the one true God. Their response was an attempt to stone him. They explained, "For a good work we stone thee not; but for blasphemy; and because that thou, being a man, makest thyself God" (John 10:33). They understood His claim but rejected it. They failed to comprehend that He was not a man making Himself God, but God who had made Himself a man (John 1:1, 14; I Timothy 3:16).

To His disciples, Jesus made His identity plain. He revealed that He was the only way to the Father and that through Him the disciples actually saw and knew the Father. "I am the way, the truth, and the life: no man cometh unto the Father, but by me. If ye had known me, ye should have known my Father also: and from henceforth ye know him, and have seen him" (John 14:6-7).

At this point Philip did not fully understand, so he asked Jesus to show them the Father. Jesus replied, "Have I been so long time with you, and yet hast thou not known me, Philip? he that hath seen me hath seen the Father; and how sayest thou then, Shew us the Father? Believest thou not that I am in the Father, and the Father in me? the words that I speak unto you I speak not of myself: but the Father that dwelleth in me, he doeth the works. Believe me that I am in the Father, and the Father in me: or else believe me for the very works' sake" (John 14:9-11).

The disciples knew that God is a Spirit, and as such He is invisible and does not have flesh and bones (John 1:18; 4:24; Luke 24:39). A human being cannot directly see the invisible Spirit; the only way he could see God is if God were to reveal Himself in some form discernible to the human senses. In other words, God would have to manifest Himself.

As Jesus pointed out to Philip, that is exactly what God did in Christ. The works of Jesus attested to His identity, for He did many acts that only God can do, such as forgiving sins, controlling the forces of nature, creating food for five thousand, and raising the dead by His own authority. Both His words and His works testified that He was God manifested in the flesh. When Philip saw Jesus, he saw God the Father in the only way that God the Father could ever be seen.

In this passage Jesus twice used a phrase similar to the language of John 14:20 and 17:21-22: "I am in the Father, and the Father in me." We have explained that those verses speak of His humanity in fellowship with God much as we can have fellowship with God and with each other. But John 14:9-11 goes beyond any human relationship to speak of the Incarnation and of Christ's identity as God: "He that hath seen me hath seen the Father. . . . The Father that dwelleth in me, he doeth the works."

We cannot say that if someone has seen us then he

has seen God, or if someone has seen us then he has seen another believer. We can say God dwells in us, but not in the unlimited way of which Christ spoke, affirming that His every word and deed was actually the authoritative word and deed of the indwelling Father. Nor can we claim that other believers dwell in us in this sense. Thus while John 14:9-11 encompasses the union of the man Jesus Christ with God, it goes beyond this concept as expressed in John 14:20 and 17:21-22 to establish the uniqueness of Christ's oneness with God. It is true that Christ related to God as other humans can and should do, but it is also true that, unlike other humans, He was actually God the Father incarnate. (See also John 1:1-14; 10:30-38; 20:28.)

Trinitarians sometimes say that Jesus was one with the Father only as two persons can be united in purpose, such as husband and wife becoming one flesh (Genesis 2:24). A husband and a wife are two persons before their union and remain two persons afterward, so when we read of them becoming "one," we know that the Bible is speaking figuratively. But the Bible never tells us that God is two or more persons, so when it repeatedly says God is one, the only one, alone, and by Himself, we understand Him to be absolutely, numerically one. (See Deuteronomy 6:4; Isaiah 44:6, 8, 24; 45:5-6.)

Moreover, as we have seen, the language of John 10:30-33 and 14:9-11 transcends even the closest possible union of two persons. The Jews in John 10 did not merely think Jesus was claiming to be in close fellowship with God; they knew He was claiming to be God. By contrast, a husband cannot claim to be his wife, or vice versa. Similarly, even the most devoted husband cannot say, "He who has seen me has seen my wife," or "The words that I speak to you I do not speak on my own authority; but my wife, who dwells in Me, does the works."

In summary, as a man Jesus was one with the Father in the same way that we can be one with God and with each other: in unity of purpose and submission. But as God, Jesus was one with the Father in a way that we cannot be: by identity and incarnation.

The Revelation of the Father

According to I John 3:1-5 the Father has revealed Himself and will reveal Himself in the person of Jesus Christ. The One acting in verse 1 is the Father: "Behold, what manner of love the Father hath bestowed upon us, that we should be called the sons of God." We are the sons of God because of the Father's love and calling. Since we are God's sons, obviously He is our Father.

The verse continues, with no change of subject, "Therefore the world knoweth us not, because it knew him not." "Him" can only mean God the Father, for there is no other possible antecedent, no other noun to which the pronoun could refer. Yet elsewhere John identified Jesus, the Word made flesh, as the One who came into the world but whom the world did not know: "He was in the world, and the world was made by him, and the world knew him not. He came unto his own, and his own received him not" (John 1:10-11).

I John 3:2 goes on to say, again without introducing any other antecedent, "Beloved, now are we the sons of God, and it doth not yet appear what we shall be: but we know that, when he shall appear, we shall be like him; for we shall see him as he is." "He" must refer back to God, who is our Father and whose sons we are. Yet elsewhere John described Jesus as the One who will appear and whom we shall see: "Behold, he cometh with clouds; and every eye shall see him, and they also which pierced him" (Revelation 1:7).

I John 3:3-5 follows: "And every man that hath this hope in him purifieth himself, even as he is pure. Whoso-ever committeth sin transgresseth also the law: for sin is the transgression of the law. And ye know that he was manifested to take away our sins; and in him is no sin." Still there is no change of antecedent. "He" still refers to God the Father. The Father "was manifested to take away our sins." Yet elsewhere John recorded that Jesus came as "the Lamb of God, which taketh away the sin of the world" (John 1:29). Jesus is the manifestation of the Father for the purpose of our salvation.

Trinitarians try to avoid this conclusion by pointing out that "he" in verses 3 and 5 comes from the Greek word *ekeinos*, literally meaning "that one." They observe that John sometimes used this demonstrative adjective to refer specifically to Christ as the "remoter antecedent," that is, when the context would otherwise point to another, closer antecedent. But the word for "him" in verses 1-2 is not *ekeinos*, but *autos*, which is the singular, masculine Greek pronoun meaning "he, him."

Moreover, in verses 3 and 5 there is a good reason to use *ekeinos*. In each case there is an intervening subject that could be mistaken as the antecedent for the pronoun, so *ekeinos* clarifies that the more remote antecedent is in view, namely, God the Father. The subject of verse 3 is "every man that hath this hope." When the verse refers back to this subject it uses *autos*, but when it wants to refer to the more remote antecedent of verse 2, which is God, it uses *ekeinos:* "And every man that hath this hope in him [*autos*, i.e., the one who hopes] purifieth himself [*eautos*, i.e., the one who hopes], even as he [*ekeinos*, i.e., God] is pure."

Likewise, the subject of verse 4 is "whosoever committeth sin," but verse 5 uses *ekeinos* so that it does not refer to this immediate antecedent. It says, "Ye know that he [*ekeinos*, i.e, God, the more remote antecedent] was manifested to take away our sins; and in him [*autos*, i.e., God, now the immediate antecedent] is no sin."

Of course, we recognize that in these verses *ekeinos* speaks of Christ, but it is important to note that in the context the antecedent is God the Father. The passage thus identifies Christ as the Father manifested to take away our sins.

For this reason, I John 2:23 can say, "Whosoever denieth the Son, the same hath not the Father: but he that acknowledgeth the Son hath the Father also." If the Father and the Son were two distinct persons, it would be theoretically possible to acknowledge one without the other. For example, the Jewish religious leaders in the first century tried to acknowledge the Father while denying the Son, Jesus Christ.

All such efforts are doomed to failure, however, because the Father has manifested Himself in His Son. If we deny that Jesus is the Son of God, that He is God manifested in the flesh, then we have not merely rejected a second person called Son, but we have rejected the Father Himself, because the Father has chosen to manifest Himself in His Son.

On the other hand, if we acknowledge that Jesus is

the Son of God, God manifested in the flesh, we do not then have to acknowledge, meet, and become acquainted with one or two additional divine persons. We have the Father also, because the Father manifested Himself in Christ. When we have a scriptural understanding of the deity of Jesus Christ, we will acknowledge the Father in Christ.

In the fullest sense, then, the Father and the Son are inseparably joined as one in Jesus Christ, the Godhead incarnate. We cannot have the Father without the Son, and vice versa. This union is not part of a trinitarian relationship; if it were, why do the scriptural descriptions consistently omit the Holy Spirit from the union? Rather this union is the consequence of the begetting of the Son and the very identity of the Son as described in chapter 6.

The Father and the Son in Believers

Jesus answered and said unto him, If a man love me, he will keep my words: and my Father will love him, and we will come unto him, and make our abode with him (John 14:23).

John 14:23 applies the union of the Father and the Son to the life of the believer. Because this verse uses plural pronouns for Jesus and the Father, trinitarians proclaim that it teaches their doctrine. Instead of teaching us about the Godhead, however, these words figuratively describe the Christian's daily experience.

Jesus promised those who love and obey Him, "We [the Father and I] will come unto him, and make our abode with him." From the context, it is clear that these words do not mean that two persons would literally inhabit or dwell inside believers. In John 14:20 Jesus said, "I am in my Father, and ye in me, and I in you." As we have already discussed, "ye in me" cannot mean that the spirit of a believer could actually fill Christ's physical body or become incarnate in Christ, but the phrase refers to communion and fellowship. The words "I in you" (verse 20) and "make our abode with him" (verse 23) similarly speak of God's having fellowship with us.

If we interpret John 14:23 to speak of two persons, then we must ask how two persons could inhabit an individual believer. They could only do so in spirit, which would require two divine spirits to live in each believer. But "there is one body, and one Spirit" (Ephesians 4:4). "For by one Spirit are we all baptized into one body, whether we be Jews or Gentiles, whether we be bond or free; and have been all made to drink into one Spirit" (I Corinthians 12:13). Christians receive only one Spirit, not two.

Therefore, both the context and other passages show that Jesus' statement in John 14:23 is metaphorical. He said that we would have both the Father and the Son, not with reference to two persons or two spirits inhabiting us, but speaking of divine characteristics that would distinguish the Christian's life.

How does the Christian actually receive these qualities into his life and thereby have fellowship with both the Father and the Son? In the same context, Jesus explained that the outpouring of the Holy Spirit would fulfill His words: "And I will pray the Father, and he shall give you another Comforter, that he may abide with you for ever. . . . I will not leave you comfortless: I will come to you. . . . But the Comforter, which is the Holy Ghost, whom the Father will send in my name, he shall teach you all things, and bring all things to your remembrance, whatsoever I have said unto you" (John 14:16, 18, 26). By receiving the one Spirit of God, we have the abiding presence of the Father and the Son.

To the person who loves God and keeps His commandments, John 14:23 promises that the Father and Son will abide with him. Elsewhere John used similar language to teach that we know we have God abiding in us because we receive His Spirit. "And he that keepeth his commandments dwelleth in him, and he in him. And hereby we know that he abideth in us, by the Spirit which he hath given us" (I John 3:24). "Hereby know we that we dwell in him, and he in us, because he hath given us of his Spirit" (I John 4:13).

When we receive the Holy Spirit we receive "the Spirit of your Father" to dwell "in" us (Matthew 10:20). The indwelling Spirit enables us to call God our Father (Romans 8:15; Galatians 4:6) and gives us access to the Father (Ephesians 2:18). When the Holy Spirit dwells in us, we have the Spirit of the Creator of the universe (Genesis 1:1-2). We have all the power of the omnipotent Father at work in our lives. The Father imparts wisdom and revelation to us, yet He does so by the Spirit (I Corinthians 2:12; 12:8; Ephesians 1:17). The Father comforts us, yet He does so by the Holy Spirit (II Corinthians 1:2-4; John 14:26). Moreover, God pours out His love in our hearts by the Holy Spirit (Romans 5:5). In sum, the Father loves us, comes to us, and makes His abode with us by filling us with His Spirit.

The Holy Spirit is also "the Spirit of his [God's] Son" (Galatians 4:6). When we receive the Holy Spirit, we specifically receive the Spirit that dwelt in Christ

(Romans 8:9-11). The Spirit led Christ continually, enabled Him to offer Himself to God, and raised Him from the dead, and the same Spirit will perform the same works in our lives (Matthew 4:1; Hebrews 9:14; Romans 8:11-14). By having "the Spirit of Jesus Christ," we can have the mind of Christ, which caused Him to be humble and obedient to the will of God even to death (Philippians 1:19; 2:5-8).

The Father strengthens us with His might by placing "his Spirit in the inner man" (Ephesians 3:16). His Spirit fills us so that "Christ may dwell in your hearts by faith" (Ephesians 3:17). The result is that "ye might be filled with all the fulness of God" (Ephesians 3:19).

In sum, believers not only enjoy the live-giving, creative, miraculous, powerful work of the Father in their lives, but they also receive the humble, submissive, obedient attitude of the Son. Truly, both the Father and the Son come to them and make their abode with them. But the Father and the Son do not come as two persons with two spirits. Nor are they two persons who somehow come via yet a third person. Believers receive both the Father and the Son when they receive the one Spirit of God. This Spirit is the eternal Father at work in our lives, and at the same time He is the Spirit of the Son.

The union of the Father and the Son is not a union of two divine persons, but it is a union of deity and humanity. This union took place in a unique way in Jesus Christ, who is both God and man at the same time. "In him dwelleth all the fulness of the Godhead bodily" (Colossians 2:9).

While no one else ever was or can be God incarnate as Jesus is, the union of Father and Son in Christ has important implications for our lives today. First, the Son was a perfect man in a perfect relationship with God, and His human life serves as the ideal model for us to emulate in our own Christian relationships. Second, the Incarnation makes available to us the divine qualities of the omnipotent Father as well as the perfect human attributes of the sinless Son. When we receive the Holy Spirit, the one Spirit of both the Father and the Son, we have everything we need to live for God.

9

The Glorification of the Son

And now, O Father, glorify thou me with thine own self with the glory which I had with thee before the world was (John 17:5).

In John 17 Jesus Christ prayed to the Father shortly before His arrest in the Garden of Gethsemane and subsequent crucifixion. He began His prayer by asking, "Father, the hour is come; glorify thy Son, that thy Son also may glorify thee" (John 17:1). In verse 5 He repeated His request for glorification and specified that He desired the glory that He had with the Father before the creation of the world.

This prayer raises a number of interesting questions. Is Jesus an inferior divinity who needs to receive glory from some other deity? Did Jesus exist as a glorified man before Creation? Are Jesus and the Father two distinct persons?

To understand this passage, we must recognize that Jesus prayed as a man. As we discussed in chapters 7 and 8, the prayers of Christ stem from His humanity, and any time we seek to interpret those prayers we must keep His humanity foremost in our minds.

Trinitarians say that Jesus was speaking as a second divine person here, but if that were so, Jesus would not be coequal with the Father, as they maintain, but inferior. Jesus would be a divine person who was lacking in glory, who needed the Father to give Him glory, and who asked the Father for help. Jesus would not be omnipotent (all powerful), but lesser in glory and power than the Father. In short, Jesus would not possess some of the essential characteristics of deity. Contrary to the rest of Scripture, He would not truly be God.

If we acknowledge that Jesus is God manifested in the flesh as the Bible teaches (Colossians 2:9; I Timothy 3:16), then we must also affirm that as God He always had divine glory, never lost it, and never needed anyone else to give it to Him. What did He mean, then, when He said, "Glorify thou me . . . with the glory which I had with thee before the world was"?

Glory through the Crucifixion and Resurrection

We can explore the setting and context for the answer. Jesus was praying in view of His upcoming crucifixion. He had come into the world to offer His life as a sacrifice for the sins of humanity (Matthew 20:28), and He realized that the time had come for Him to fulfill this plan. Although His humanity naturally shrank from the upcoming agony, He knew that His death on the cross was the supreme, perfect will of God for Him. As He had said earlier in John 12:27, contemplating His death, "Now My soul is troubled, and what shall I say? 'Father, save Me from this hour'? But for this purpose I came to this hour" (NKJV).

The glory to which Jesus referred in John 17:1, 5 is therefore predicated upon His submitting as a man to the plan of God through the crucifixion, resurrection, and ascension. Immediately after the statement of John 12:27 Jesus prayed, "Father, glorify thy name. Then came there a voice from heaven, saying, I have both glorified it, and will glorify it again" (John 12:28). Jesus then explained, "And I, if I be lifted up from the earth, will draw all men unto me. This he said, signifying what death he should die" (John 12:32-33). God glorified Christ by lifting Him up before all the world on the cross.

God further glorified Christ by raising Him from the dead. "Christ was raised up from the dead by the glory of the Father" (Romans 6:4). Christ's atoning death became effective for us by His resurrection (Romans 4:25), which transformed His death into victory over sin, the devil, and death itself. At His resurrection He received a glorified human body (Philippians 3:21).

God glorified the man Jesus throughout His earthly ministry by investing Him with divine power and working through Him miraculously, but the supreme glorification occurred through the death and resurrection of Jesus Christ. That was the ultimate plan for which Jesus was born and lived.

The eternal glory of God is not, therefore, the subject of discussion in John 17, but the glory the man Jesus Christ received by fulfilling God's plan for our salvation.

Jesus said of His disciples in John 17:22 that they shared in the glory that God gave to Him: "And the glory which thou gavest me I have given them; that they may be one, even as we are one." God emphatically declares that He will never share His *divine* glory with anyone else. "My glory will I not give to another" (Isaiah 42:8). "I will not give my glory unto another" (Isaiah 48:11). Jesus could not have meant that He gave the disciples the glory of deity.

Instead, He referred to the glory that He as a man received in fulfilling God's plan of salvation for the human race, the benefits of which He imparts to those who believe in Him. The disciples had already shared in Christ's glorious, miraculous ministry. Soon they would also share in the glory of His crucifixion and resurrection by receiving the Holy Spirit (I Peter 1:11-12). They would have "Christ in you, the hope of glory" (Colossians 1:27), an experience that would be "joy unspeakable and full of glory" (I Peter 1:8). Through the gospel, people obtain "the glory of our Lord Jesus Christ" (II Thessalonians 2:14). By "the salvation which is in Christ Jesus" we have "eternal glory" (II Timothy 2:10).

Another day of glory also awaits believers, for when He returns we will "be found unto praise and honour and glory at the appearing of Jesus Christ" (I Peter 1:7). Just as God glorified the man Christ by raising Him from the dead with an immortal body, so we will be "raised in glory" (I Corinthians 15:42-43). In our resurrection, we will receive a glorified body "like unto his glorious body" (Philippians 3:21). We will be "glorified together" with Him (Romans 8:17), and we shall "appear with him in glory" (Colossians 3:4).

The end result of God's plan of salvation is that believers will live with the glorified Christ throughout eternity. They will behold His glory, and will worship Him as the glorified One. They will say, "Worthy is the Lamb that was slain to receive power, and riches, and wisdom, and strength, and honour, and glory, and blessing" (Revelation 5:12). With this ultimate objective in mind, Christ prayed, "Father, I will that they also, whom thou hast given me, be with me where I am; that they may behold my glory, which thou hast given me: for thou lovedst me before the foundation of the world" (John 17:24).

Foreordained Glory

Knowing that the human race would fall into sin, God foreordained a plan of salvation based on the birth, death, and resurrection of the Son of God. "Forasmuch as ye know that ye were not redeemed with corruptible things, as silver and gold, from your vain conversation received by tradition from your fathers; but with the precious blood of Christ, as of a lamb without blemish and without spot: who verily was foreordained before the foundation of the world, but was manifest in these last times for you" (I Peter 1:18-20). Jesus is "the Lamb slain from the foundation of the world" (Revelation 13:8).

Jesus Christ was not actually born before the creation of the world, nor was He actually crucified at that time. But in the plan of God the atoning sacrifice of Christ was a foreordained, certain event. God does not inhabit time as we do; the past, present, and future are all alike to Him. He "calleth those things which be not as though they were" (Romans 4:17). As discussed in chapter 4, He created the world with the Son in view, predicating all creation upon the future arrival and atonement of the Son of God.

When Jesus asked for the Father to give Him the glory He had with Him before the world began, He was not speaking of a time when He lived alongside the Father as a second divine person. Glory from such a time would be divine glory, which He could never have lost and which He could never share with His disciples.

Before the Incarnation, the Spirit of Jesus was the one eternal God, not a second person. The glory of which Jesus spoke was the glory He as a man would have in the fulfillment of God's foreordained plan of redemption for the human race. That was what Jesus looked forward to as He prayed, and that was what He asked the Father to give Him so that He could share it with all believers.

The Glorification of the Name

Jesus asked for glory so that He could in turn glorify the Father, and He also affirmed that He had already glorified the Father (John 17:1, 4). Throughout His earthly ministry He exalted God through His teachings and through the miracles He performed. But He knew that the supreme glorification of the Father would take place through His crucifixion and resurrection. His crucifixion would reveal God's love in an unparalleled way (Romans 5:8), and His resurrection would supremely demonstrate God's almighty power (Ephesians 1:19-20).

Jesus prayed, "Father, glorify thy name" (John 12:28). In the context, the subject of discussion was Christ's death. Jesus wanted God to glorify the divine name through Christ's own life and death.

God's name represents His character, power, authority, and abiding presence. (See Exodus 6:3-7; 9:16; 23:20-

21; I Kings 8:29, 43.) Jesus thus requested that God's character and presence be revealed through His human life.

In John 17, Jesus stated that He had indeed revealed God's name, that is, God's character and presence, to His disciples. "I have manifested thy name unto the men which thou gavest me out of the world. . . . I kept them in thy name. . . . I have declared unto them thy name, and will declare it" (John 17:6, 12, 26). In short, Christ revealed the Father to us. To put it another way, in Christ the Father revealed Himself.

In John 17:11, Jesus prayed, "Holy Father, keep through thine own name those whom thou hast given me." Interestingly, most scholars conclude today that in the original Greek text the word translated as "those" is actually in the singular rather than the plural. If so, the meaning would be, "Holy Father, protect them by the power of your name—the name you gave me" (NIV).

This reading would correspond to other statements in Scripture that Jesus bears the Father's name. Jesus said, "I am come in my Father's name" (John 5:43). Hebrews 1:4 says of the Son, "He hath by inheritance obtained a more excellent name." Since the Son inherited His name, it must have first belonged to His Father.

The name that the Son of God received was Jesus (Matthew 1:21). It was the name He bore all His life, and the name that was broadcast throughout the country as a result of His miracles and teachings. It was the name given credit for the miracles in the early church (Acts 3:6, 16). It is the only name in which we receive salvation and remission of sins (Acts 4:12; 10:43).

When we invoke the name of Jesus in faith, all the power and authority of God becomes available to us.

Moreover, when God answers prayers offered in the name of Jesus, the Father is glorified in His Son. "And whatsoever ye shall ask in my name, that will I do, that the Father may be glorified in the Son. If ye shall ask any thing in my name, I will do it" (John 14:13-14).

The Father has chosen to reveal Himself to this world by the name of Jesus, which literally means "Jehovah-Savior" or "Jehovah Is Salvation." The Father glorified the man Jesus by investing His name (character, power, authority, presence) in Him, by leading Him to the cross to die for the sins of the world, and by raising Him from the dead. Far from manifesting to us a second person of the Godhead unknown to Old Testament saints, the Son manifested to us the one, indivisible God for the purpose of our salvation.

10

The Right Hand of God

The Bible teaches that God is an invisible Spirit, yet it also describes Him in terms that relate to the human body. Many trinitarians use these descriptions to support their doctrine, particularly passages that speak of the right hand of God and the face of God. Let us investigate what the Bible means by these terms.

John 4:24 says, "God is a Spirit," or "God is spirit" (NIV). This means His eternal essence is not human or physical. Apart from the Incarnation, God does not have a physical body. "A spirit hath not flesh and bones" (Luke 24:39). God the Father is not "flesh and blood" (Matthew 16:17).

Because He is a Spirit, God is invisible to humans. "No man hath seen God at any time" (John 1:18). "No man hath seen, nor can see" Him (I Timothy 6:16).

Moreover, the Bible teaches that God is omnipresent: His Spirit fills the universe. "Whither shall I go from thy spirit? or whither shall I flee from thy presence? If I ascend up into heaven, thou art there: if I make my bed in hell, behold, thou art there. If I take the wings of the morning, and dwell in the uttermost parts of the sea; even there shall thy hand lead me, and thy right hand shall hold me" (Psalm 139:7-10).

These facts about God show that we cannot understand the physical descriptions of Him in a grossly "letteristic" way. We are to interpret the Bible according to the ordinary, apparent, grammatical, historical meaning of its words, just as we do with other forms of speech and writing. In doing so, we will recognize that all human communication, including the Bible, uses figurative language. We are not free to impose an allegorical interpretation upon Scripture, but when the Bible itself indicates that we are to understand certain phrases or passages in a figurative way, then that is how we must interpret them.

When we read about God's eyes, nostrils, heart, feet, hands, and wings, it is clear from the rest of Scripture that we are not dealing with a human, beast, or fowl. The Bible does not use these terms to describe a physical being, but to give us insight into the nature, character, and attributes of God. For instance, God expresses His sovereignty by saying, "The heaven is my throne, and the earth is my footstool" (Isaiah 66:1). The Bible describes God's miraculous power as "the finger of God" and "the blast of thy nostrils" (Exodus 8:19; 15:8); His omniscience and omnipresence by saying, "The eyes of the LORD are in every place" (Proverbs 15:3); His protection by speaking of "the shadow of thy wings" (Psalm 36:7); and His sorrow over human sin as having "grieved him at his heart" (Genesis 6:6).

It would be foolish to conclude from these passages that God is a giant who props up His feet on the North Pole, blows air from His nostrils, focuses his eyes to see us, uses wings to fly, and has a blood-pumping organ. Rather the Bible uses concepts taken from our human experience to enable us to understand the characteristics of God's spiritual nature.

The Significance of the Right Hand

This principle is especially true when the Bible speaks of the right hand of God. Since most humans are right-handed, in most cultures the right hand signifies strength, skill, and dexterity. The very word *dexterity* comes from the Latin word *dexter*, meaning "on the right side." In ancient times, the most honored guest was seated on the right hand of the host. As a result, in Hebrew, Greek, and English the right hand is a metaphor for power and honor.

The Bible uses this metaphor repeatedly with reference to humans as well as God. Of course, in some passages the Bible uses "right" or "right hand" in its locational meaning, in contrast to "left" or "left hand." But many times the use of "right hand" is figurative. Since God does not have a physical right hand (apart from the Incarnation) and is not confined to a physical location, when the Bible speaks of His right hand, it speaks figuratively or metaphorically.

A study of the "right hand" passages in the Bible reveals that the right hand of God represents His almighty *power*, His omnipotence, particularly in bestowing *salva-*

tion, deliverance, victory, and preservation. "My right hand hath spanned the heavens" (Isaiah 48:13). "Thy right hand, O LORD, is become glorious in power: thy right hand, O LORD, hath dashed in pieces the enemy. . . . Thou stretchedst out thy right hand, the earth swallowed them" (Exodus 15:6, 12). "His right hand, and his holy arm, hath gotten him the victory" (Psalm 98:1). "Thy right hand shall save me" (Psalm 138:7). "I will uphold thee with the right hand of my righteousness" (Isaiah 41:10). There are numerous other examples where the Bible uses "right hand" as a metaphor for power.[1]

In Scripture, the right hand also signifies the *position of honor, blessing, and preeminence.* "At thy right hand there are pleasures for evermore" (Psalm 16:11). "Thy right hand is full of righteousness" (Psalm 48:10). "A wise man's heart is at his right hand; but a fool's heart at his left" (Ecclesiastes 10:2).

When Jacob blessed Joseph's two sons, Joseph wanted him to put his right hand upon Manasseh, the older son, to signify that he would have preeminence. Joseph insisted, "This is the firstborn; put thy right hand upon his head" (Genesis 48:18). Jacob refused, in a reversal of normal procedure, saying, "Truly his younger brother shall be greater than he" (Genesis 48:19). (For other examples where the right hand means a position of favor or preeminence, see Exodus 29:20; Leviticus 8:23; 14:14-28; Psalm 45:9; 110:1; Jeremiah 22:24; Matthew 25:33-34.)

Jesus at the Right Hand of God

So then after the Lord had spoken unto them, he was received up into heaven, and sat on the right hand of God (Mark 16:19).

Many passages in the New Testament tell us that Jesus sits on the right hand of God. As we have already seen, it would be a mistake to interpret this description to mean that Jesus sits eternally on top of a giant divine hand or at the side of another divine personage. How could we determine what is the right hand of the omnipresent Spirit of God?

The obvious purpose of this description is to exalt the Lord Jesus Christ. By using this phrase, the New Testament tells us that Jesus is not merely a man, but He is a man who has been invested with the almighty power of the indwelling Spirit of God and who has been exalted to the position of highest honor.

Since verses like Mark 16:19 speak of Jesus as being "on the right hand of God," some people suppose that in heaven they will see two divine persons, the Father and the Son, sitting or standing side by side. But no one has ever seen or can see God's invisible presence (I Timothy 6:16); no one can see God apart from Christ. Moreover, God has emphatically declared that there is no one beside Him (Isaiah 43:11; 44:6, 8). Christ is the visible "image of the invisible God," and the only way we can see the Father is to see Him (Colossians 1:15; John 14:9). There is only one divine throne in heaven, and only One on that throne (Revelation 4:2; 22:3-4). As chapter 11 discusses, that One is Jesus.

New Testament passages make clear that Jesus is "on the right hand of God" in the sense of having divine power, honor, glory, and preeminence. Jesus Himself said, "Hereafter shall ye see the Son of man sitting on the right hand of power, and coming in the clouds of heaven" (Matthew 26:64). "Hereafter shall the Son of man sit on the right hand of the power of God" (Luke 22:69). These words do not imply that we will see two divine persons in the clouds or in heaven, but one divine-human person who has all the power and glory of the invisible Spirit of God.

Jesus was "by the right hand of God exalted" (Acts 2:33). He "is gone into heaven, and is on the right hand of God; angels and authorities and powers being made subject unto him" (I Peter 3:22). God "raised him [Christ] from the dead, and set him at his own right hand in the heavenly places, far above all principality, and power, and might, and dominion, and every name that is named, not only in this world, but also in that which is to come" (Ephesians 1:20-21). "If ye then be risen with Christ, seek those things which are above, where Christ sitteth on the right hand of God" (Colossians 3:1).

When Stephen was stoned, he "saw the glory of God, and Jesus standing on the right hand of God" (Acts 7:55). He did not see two personages, but he saw the glory of God surrounding Jesus, who was revealed in the position of supreme power and authority. While on earth Jesus appeared to be an ordinary man and He lived as such with His disciples, but after His resurrection and ascension He appeared with visible glory and power as the almighty God. Although John had been Christ's closest associate while He was on earth and knew Him well, when he saw the ascended Christ in a vision he "fell at his feet as dead" (Revelation 1:17). Unlike Christ's typical appearance on earth, John saw Him in His divine glory.

That is what Stephen beheld also. The only divine person he saw was Jesus, and the only divine person he addressed was Jesus. He said, "Behold, I see the heavens opened, and the Son of man standing on the right hand of

God" (Acts 7:56). He died "calling upon God, and saying, Lord Jesus, receive my spirit" (Acts 7:59).

F. F. Bruce, one of the foremost evangelical theologians of the twentieth century, explained that biblical scholars past and present recognize Christ's right-hand position to be metaphoric, not physical:

> Christ's present position of supremacy is described in the Pauline writings as being "at the right hand of God." . . . The apostles knew very well that they were using figurative language when they spoke of Christ's exaltation in these terms: they no more thought of a location on a literal throne at God's literal right hand than their twentieth-century successors do. . . . Martin Luther satirizes "that heaven of the fanatics . . . with its golden chair and Christ seated at the Father's side, vested in a choir cope and a golden robe, as the painters love to portray him!"[2]

Several passages carry a further connotation relative to Christ's right-hand position: they use this term to describe His present mediatorial role. "It is Christ that died, yea rather, that is risen again, who is even at the right hand of God, who also maketh intercession for us" (Romans 8:34).

This does not mean that Christ has been kneeling for two thousand years, praying to some other deity. As a man, He has been glorified and has no further need to pray. As God, He never needed to pray and never had anyone to whom He could pray. Moreover, there is nothing He needs to add to the Atonement; His one sacrifice on the cross is sufficient to cover the sins of the whole world. When He said, "It is finished" and then died, His atoning work was complete (John 19:30). He "offered one sacrifice for sins for ever" (Hebrews 10:12).

What Christ's present intercession means is that His sacrifice is continually effective in our lives. His blood can cover our sins today. If we sin, we still have "an advocate with the Father, Jesus Christ the righteous" (I John 2:1). When we confess our sins to God, no one needs to convince Him to forgive us; He looks at the Cross, and that event is all the advocacy we need.

To remind us that Christ was a real man who died for our sins and so became our advocate, mediator, and high priest, the New Testament speaks of Him as at the "right hand of God." At the same time, it shows us the completeness and finality of His work on the cross by saying that after His mediatorial work, He "sat down" on the right hand. "When he had by himself purged our sins, sat down on the right hand of the Majesty on high" (Hebrews 1:3). "We have such an high priest, who is set on the right hand of the throne of the Majesty in the heavens" (Hebrews 8:1). "But this man, after he had offered one sacrifice for sins for ever, sat down on the right hand of God" (Hebrews 10:12). Jesus "is set down at the right hand of the throne of God" (Hebrews 12:2).

Significantly, the Book of Revelation never describes Jesus as being on the right hand of God. It looks forward to the time when His mediatorial role will no longer be necessary. In eternity to come, we will not see Him in the right-hand position as an exalted man who serves as our mediator, but we will see Him as the One on the throne, the One who is both God and the Lamb at the same time (Revelation 22:3-4).

The Wycliffe Bible Commentary explains the significance of Christ's right-hand position and its reference to the present age:

> The position occupied by Christ [is] the place of authority and of priestly service. For believers, he both rules and intercedes. . . . The rule of Christ will become actual. Meanwhile he patiently waits for the time when his enemies will be vanquished. There will then be no more opposition to Christ or his rule.[3]

The Face of God

Take heed that ye despise not one of these little ones; for I say unto you, That in heaven their angels do always behold the face of my Father which is in heaven (Matthew 18:10).

Based on Matthew 18:10, some suppose that one person of God resided in heaven while Jesus was a second person on earth. Such a notion fails to consider that God is an omnipresent, invisible Spirit. While Jesus Christ walked on earth as God manifested in the flesh, the Spirit of God still filled the universe and ruled from heaven. While the complete personality of God was incarnate in Christ (Colossians 2:9), His Spirit could not be confined to any physical location. However, this fact does not mean that God consists of two or more personalities or centers of consciousness.

As we have already seen about other bodily terms used in relation to God, it would be a mistake to interpret God's "face" to refer to a physical body apart from Christ. In the Bible, "face" is often used as a metaphor for someone's *attention, favor, and presence.*

Jacob fled "from the face of Esau" his brother (Genesis 35:1). The Lord destroyed the enemies of the Israelites before their face (Deuteronomy 8:20; 9:3). God said He would hide His face from Israel because of their sins (Deuteronomy 31:17). When King Jeroboam requested that a prophet pray for his healing, he said, "Entreat now the face of the Lord thy God" (I Kings 13:6). The psalmist prayed, "God be merciful unto us, and bless us; and cause his face to shine upon us" (Psalm 67:1). (See also II Chronicles 30:9; Psalm 10:11; 27:9; 80:3, 7, 19; Isaiah 59:2; Jeremiah 44:11; Ezekiel 39:29; Daniel 9:17.)

As Vine's *Expository Dictionary of New Testament Words* notes, *prosopon*, the Greek word translated "face" in Matthew 18:10, often refers to "the presence of a person, the face being the noblest part."[4] For instance, Acts 3:13 says that the Jewish rulers denied Jesus "in the presence *[prosopon]* of Pilate." In Acts 5:41, the disciples "departed from the presence *[prosopon]* of the council."

The angels are spirit beings and do not need to perceive God in a physical fashion. It is impossible for us to know how they discern, relate to, and communicate with God in the spiritual realm. When the Bible says they behold His face, it does not refer to human senses, but it uses human terms to describe their spiritual interaction.

Matthew 18:10 does not mean that the angels are stationed eternally in a physical location in front of a physical image of God. If they were, how could they assist God's children on earth, as the passages implies? As *The Tyndale New Testament Commentaries* explains, Matthew 18:10 simply means that the angels "have access at all times to the Father's presence."[5]

The Throne of God

To him that overcometh will I grant to sit with me in my throne, even as I also overcame, and am set down with my Father in his throne (Revelation 3:21).

The Bible speaks of thrones in both literal and metaphorical senses. The throne of a king may mean the actual chair he sits upon, or it may represent his kingdom or reign. Colossians 1:16 speaks of "thrones" in the sense of powers or authorities. Jesus has inherited "the throne of his father David"—not a golden chair, but the position and right to be king of Israel (Luke 1:32).

The Bible teaches that God is the Sovereign of the universe by describing Him as sitting upon a throne. The Book of Revelation indicates that in heaven we will actually see God and the Lamb (one being) sitting upon a throne (Revelation 22:3-4), but we should not suppose that the Spirit of God is somehow confined to a physical throne throughout eternity. The Bible says that heaven is God's throne and earth is His footstool (Isaiah 66:1), and it also says that Jerusalem shall be called His throne (Jeremiah 3:17). Clearly, then, God's throne represents His sovereignty without necessary reference to a physical chair.

In Revelation 3:21, Jesus said, "I . . . am set down with my Father in his throne." If we interpret this statement to refer to two divine persons with two bodies, then two persons would be sitting in one throne, a direct contradiction of Revelation 4:2. Clearly, this is not the intention of the verse. Rather, it expresses that the man Jesus has been exalted by the indwelling Spirit to the position of highest authority in the universe. God rules from heaven as the incarnate One, Jesus Christ.

Saying that Jesus sits in the Father's throne means essentially the same as saying that Jesus sits at the right hand of God, if we interpret both descriptions metaphorically, as we have suggested. If we interpret both statements in a strictly literal fashion, however, we have a biblical contradiction. We have Jesus sitting in the Father's throne, but Hebrews 8:1 and 12:2 state that He is sitting "on the right hand of the throne of the Majesty in the heavens" and "is set down at the right hand of the throne of God." He cannot be sitting in the throne and at the right side of the throne at the same time.

Jesus also promised in Revelation 3:21, "To him that overcometh will I grant to sit with me in my throne." We must interpret this part of the verse as metaphorical, just as the rest of the verse, since a literal interpretation would place millions of believers sitting in the throne with Jesus—either beside Him or on Him. Instead, we must understand Jesus to mean that He will share His power and authority with believers, so that they will rule with Him.

Indeed, the saints in Revelation proclaim that the Lamb has "made us unto our God kings and priests: and we shall reign on the earth" (Revelation 5:10). In the millennial kingdom, the saints receive thrones from which to judge the nations (Revelation 20:4). As an Old Testament example of this type of metaphor, I Samuel 2:8 says that God will enable the poor to "inherit the throne of glory."

There is only one divine throne in heaven, and One sits on that throne (Revelation 4:2). While Revelation 3:21 can say metaphorically that the saints will sit on Christ's throne, we must realize that they will not share God's divine glory or sovereignty. When God's sovereignty over heaven and earth throughout eternity is in view, it is clear that the saints are before the throne, not on it. "The four and twenty elders and the four beasts fell down and worshipped God that sat on the throne, saying, Amen; Alleluia" (Revelation 19:4).

In studying this subject, it is helpful to realize that when the Bible talks about humans sitting on God's throne, it means the throne He has prepared for them. For example, the queen of Sheba told Solomon, "Blessed be the LORD thy God, which delighted in thee to set thee on his throne, to be king for the LORD thy God" (II Chronicles 9:8). Solomon sat on God's throne—not taking over God's position as King of the universe, but occupying the position of authority that God had ordained for him.

Confession before the Father

He that overcometh, the same shall be clothed in white raiment; and I will not blot out his name out of the book of life, but I will confess his name before my Father, and before his angels (Revelation 3:5).

Some people take Revelation 3:5 to mean that in the judgment Jesus will appear as our spokesman or advocate before another divine person. Once again, however, this is an erroneous interpretation based on the mistaken notion that we can see God in a physical body apart from Christ.

The statement of Revelation 3:5 is reminiscent of Christ's teaching in the Gospels: "Whosoever therefore shall confess me before men, him will I confess also before my Father which is in heaven" (Matthew 10:32). "Also I say unto you, Whosoever shall confess me before men, him shall the Son of man also confess before the angels of God" (Luke 12:8).

These verses are not speaking of advocacy before another person at the last judgment, for two reasons. First, angels will have no position of judgment over humans. Instead, redeemed humans will judge angels (I Corinthians 6:3).

Second, the Bible teaches that Jesus Christ will be the judge of everyone in the last day. "For the Father judgeth no man, but hath committed all judgment unto the Son" (John 5:22). "We must all appear before the judgment seat of Christ" (II Corinthians 5:10). "God shall judge the secrets of men by Jesus Christ" (Romans 2:16). Jesus will be the One on the throne who will judge the human race. He will do so as God, but as God who came in flesh, experienced the same temptations that we do, gave us a perfect example to follow, and provided the sacrifice of atonement to deliver us from sin.

How, then, does Jesus confess us before the Father and the angels? First, He does so by being our mediator and by searching our hearts in this life. We who believe and obey His gospel have His blood to cover our lives. On the basis of Christ's mediatorial role we are accepted by God, and our redeemed status is made known to the angels.

Second, Christ will complete the work of redemption by transforming us into His sinless, glorified, perfect likeness (Philippians 3:20-21; I John 3:2). In the end time, He will proclaim our status by presenting "to himself a glorious church, not having spot, or wrinkle, or any such thing" (Ephesians 5:27).

In sum, Christ's statement in Revelation 3:5 assures us of "the heavenly standing of those who belong to Christ. . . . [It] means that in highest heaven this man has nothing to fear. When Jesus Christ vouches for a man he is accepted."[6] In the words of Romans 8:34: "Who is he that condemneth? It is Christ that died, yea rather, that is risen again, who is even at the right hand of God, who also maketh intercession for us."

Just as Christ is not continually praying on our behalf before some other divine being, so He will not plead our case before some other divine being in the life to come. Instead, His sacrifice stands before the justice of God to plead our case both now and in the judgment. If we confess Him now, then by His sacrifice on our behalf, He will confess us both now and in the judgment. In the sight of God and His holy angels we will be redeemed by the blood of Jesus Christ.

11

Whom Will We See in Heaven?

"If God is a trinity, how many thrones are there in heaven, and whom will we see there?" asked a curious student in the religion class.

"You know, I've never thought about that. The Bible doesn't really say," replied the lecturer, an ordained denominational minister.

I could not believe my ears! An acknowledged theological expert was confessing his ignorance of a basic Bible fact about his God. I raised my hand to respond and then read John's inspired words in Revelation 4:2: "And immediately I was in the spirit: and, behold, a throne was set in heaven, and one sat on the throne."

"The Bible does give us the answer. There is only one throne in heaven, and those who go there will see only one God on the throne," I concluded.

"Well, you've offered powerful support for your position," the teacher conceded as the class period ended.

Such confusion about the God they expect to see in heaven is by no means unusual among trinitarians. Bernard Ramm, a leading evangelical theologian, sidestepped the issue in his *Protestant Biblical Interpretation:* "Many are the questions asked about heaven. . . . Will we see the Trinity or just the Son? . . . Where Scripture has not spoken, we are wisest to remain silent."[1]

Trinitarians try to resolve the tension between the many scriptural assertions of God's absolute oneness and their affirmation of plurality in the Godhead by reciting that God is "three in one." When accused of tritheism, they indignantly insist, "Oh no! We believe in one God." When asked if Jesus is the incarnation of all the Godhead, however, they maintain that He is not, for their "one" God exists mysteriously as three distinct persons.

While the concept of "three in one" may be a convenient philosophical concept on earth, it does not provide much help in answering the question, "Whom will we see in heaven?" To answer "three in one" is unsatisfactory, for how can anyone see "three in one"?

If a trinitarian answers that he will see three, then he is a tritheist—a believer in three separate and distinct gods—despite his protestations to the contrary. If there is a trinity of persons with separate bodies, each of whom can interact with us individually, then they are not one God in any meaningful sense.

On the other hand, if a trinitarian answers that he will see only one God, then the next question is, "Who will He be?" A study of Scripture shows that the One we will see is Jesus Christ, and once a person agrees to that proposition he has essentially adopted the Oneness position.

Revelation 4:8 describes the One on the throne as "Holy, holy, holy, Lord God Almighty, which was, and is, and is to come." This Lord is our Lord Jesus Christ, for Revelation 1 has already described Jesus in identical terms: "Behold, he cometh with clouds; and every eye shall see him, and they also which pierced him: and all kindreds of the earth shall wail because of him. Even so, Amen. I am Alpha and Omega, the beginning and the ending, saith the Lord, which is, and which was, and which is to come, the Almighty. . . . I am Alpha and Omega, the first and the last. . . . I am the first and the last: I am he that liveth, and was dead; and, behold, I am alive for evermore" (Revelation 1:7-8, 11, 17-18).

As evidence of two separate divine persons in heaven, trinitarians often point to Revelation 5, which describes the One on the throne and the Lamb. "The Lion of the tribe of Juda" appeared to John as a Lamb, and this Lamb took a book from the right hand of the One on the throne. This vision is clearly symbolic, for we do not expect to see a literal lion or lamb in heaven. John's vision of the Lamb was a symbolic depiction of the Incarnation and the Atonement. The Lamb represented the Son of God, particularly His sacrificial role (John 1:29). The Lamb is not a second divine person but the man Jesus Christ, for the Lamb was slain, and only humanity—not deity—can die.

The *Pulpit Commentary*, although written by trinitarians, concedes this point. It identifies the One on the throne as the Triune God, and it identifies the Lamb as Christ in His human capacity only.[2] Thus it does not interpret this vision of the Lamb to mean a separate divine person.

The Lamb had "seven eyes, which are the seven Spirits of God." Seven is the number of perfection and completion, so the seven eyes represent the fullness of the Holy Spirit. Thus the Holy Spirit is not a third person, separate from the Lamb, but is the Spirit dwelling in the Lamb that He "sent forth into all the earth" (Revelation 5:6).

The Lamb is not a separate person from the One on the throne; rather, the Lamb actually came out of the throne. "And I beheld, and, lo, in the midst of the throne, and of the four beasts, and in the midst of the elders, stood a Lamb" (Revelation 5:6). Some translations by trinitarians say merely that the Lamb was in front of the throne, but the lexicon of Bauer, Arndt, Gingrich, and Danker, the most widely used and respected dictionary of New Testament Greek, says the Lamb stood "on the center of the throne and among the four living creatures."[3] Other translations also show that the Lamb was actually on the throne: "Then, I saw a Lamb . . . standing in the center of the throne, encircled by the four living creatures and the elders" (NIV). "Then, standing in the very center of the throne and of the four living creatures and of the Elders, I saw a Lamb" (Phillips).

Revelation 7:17 describes the Lamb as sitting on the throne: "the Lamb which is in the midst of the throne" (KJV); "the Lamb at the center of the throne" (NIV); "the Lamb who is in the center of the throne" (Phillips). Again, Bauer et al. are very clear as to the meaning of the Greek: "the lamb who is (seated) on the center of the throne."

A beautiful truth emerges: the one God who sits on

the throne became the Lamb. Our Creator became our Savior. Our Father is our Redeemer (Isaiah 63:16). God did not demonstrate His great love for us by sending someone else; instead, He came Himself and He gave of Himself. "To wit, that God was in Christ, reconciling the world unto himself" (II Corinthians 5:19).

The Lamb is the One God incarnate, not a second person. Revelation 21:22 says that "the Lord God Almighty and the Lamb are the temple" of the New Jerusalem. In the Greek, the verb is singular, literally saying, "the Lord God Almighty and the Lamb is the temple." Revelation 22:3 speaks of "the throne of God and of the Lamb," clearly identifying it as one throne for one being, not two thrones. By using singular personal pronouns, the next verse shows that "God and the Lamb" is one person: "And his servants shall serve him: and they shall see his face; and his name shall be in their foreheads" (Revelation 22:4).

Who is this One called both God and the Lamb? Only one being is both sovereign and sacrifice, both deity and humanity—Jesus Christ. No one has ever seen God at any time except by manifestation or incarnation (I John 4:12), so what face will we see? The face of Jesus Christ, the express image of the invisible God (Colossians 1:15; Hebrews 1:3). And whose name will we bear? The only saving name, the highest name ever given, the name at which every knee shall bow and every tongue shall confess—Jesus Christ (Acts 4:12; Philippians 2:9-11).

When we arrive in heaven we will see one God on the throne—Jesus Christ. We will recognize in Him our Father, Savior, and Holy Spirit, for "in him dwelleth all the fulness of the Godhead bodily" (Colossians 2:9). If someone expects or desires to see other divine persons, he should ponder Christ's words to Philip: "He that hath seen me hath seen the Father; and how sayest thou then, Shew us the Father?" (John 14:9).

We do not have to be confused about the One to whom we pray, whom we worship, and whom we will meet in heaven. In the words of Titus 2:13 (NKJV), let us look for the "glorious appearing of our great God and Savior Jesus Christ."

Appendix A

The True Doctrinal Views of the United Pentecostal Church on the Godhead

In a newsletter, Walter Martin, the self-styled Bible Answer Man and a radio speaker who specializes in identifying cults, called the United Pentecostal Church International (UPCI) "the fastest growing of all the cultic structures" and "certainly one of the most dangerous." Normally, such an extreme attack merits no comment, but the surprising amount of misinformation accompanying this remarkable assertion needs to be pointed out.

The newsletter declares that "the most lethal danger" of the UPCI is "the Jesus Only doctrine which states that there is no Trinity; that the Father, Son, and the Holy Spirit are only titles for Jesus." This definition of the Oneness position is simplistic, misleading, and inaccurate.

First, the UPCI does not use the label "Jesus Only," because it may erroneously imply a denial of the Father and the Holy Spirit. Second, the UPCI teaches that the one God existed as Father and Holy Spirit before His incarnation as Jesus Christ, the Son of God, and that while Jesus walked on earth as God Himself incarnate, the Spirit of God continued to be omnipresent. We affirm that God has revealed Himself as Father (in parental relationship to humanity), in the Son (in human flesh), and as the Holy Spirit (in action).

We do not accept the trinitarian concept of three distinct centers of consciousness in the Godhead, but we hold that God is absolutely and indivisibly one (Deuteronomy 6:4; Galatians 3:20). Moreover, we affirm that in Jesus dwells all the fullness of the Godhead bodily (Colossians 2:9) and that Jesus is the only name given for salvation (Acts 4:12). The Father is revealed to us in the name of Jesus, the Son was given the name of Jesus at birth, and the Holy Spirit comes to us in the name of Jesus (Matthew 1:21; John 5:43; 14:26; 17:6). Thus the apostles correctly fulfilled Christ's command to baptize "in the name [singular] of the Father, and of the Son, and of the Holy Ghost" (Matthew 28:19) by baptizing all converts in the name of Jesus (Acts 2:38; 8:16; 10:48; 19:5; 22:16).

The newsletter also errs historically: "The 'United Pentecostal' or 'Jesus Only' church was disfellowshipped and deemed a non-Christian cult by the Assemblies of God in 1916." The UPC did not come into existence until 1945. In 1916 the Assemblies of God adopted a strong, detailed trinitarian statement that caused Oneness preachers to leave the two-year-old organization. Some trinitarian preachers left also, because the church had violated its founding principle of adopting no creed other than the Bible. Those who remained in the Assemblies of God felt that the Oneness believers were in doctrinal error, but at no time did they classify them as a non-Christian cult. To the contrary, books and personal interviews from both sides reveal that the trinitarian majority was saddened by the loss of those whom it considered to be mistaken brethren, and Oneness ministers preached for Assemblies of God churches long after the split.

In any case, do the doctrinal teachings and ministerial requirements of the Assemblies of God determine whether or not a group is a cult? No one can be a preacher in that denomination unless he has received the Holy Ghost with the evidence of speaking in tongues; does it follow, then, that all non-Pentecostal groups are cults? Moreover, the Roman Catholic Church, which has a far greater history and membership than the Assemblies of God, officially excommunicated the Protestants, consigning them to damnation. Does this action mean that all Protestants are cultists? We can only appeal to the Bible, not a denomination, to determine whether a doctrine is true or false.

The newsletter further claims, "In John 10:30 the original Greek has Jesus saying: 'I and my Father, *we* are in union'" (emphasis is Martin's), describing this verse as "devastating" to the Oneness position. But no major translation of the Bible adopts this rendering. The King James Version says, "I and my Father are one." The Greek word *hen* in this verse is the first cardinal number (neuter form). Like the English word *one*, *hen* can sometimes have the connotation of unity, but its fundamental meaning and translation is simply "one." Moreover, the Greek preposition for "in" does not appear in this verse. Saying that *hen* means "in union" instead of "one" is a theological interpretation, not a direct translation from the Greek.

Moreover, there is no reason to supply and emphasize the word *we*. It is true that every Greek verb indicates the person and number of its subject. Thus, John 10:30 uses the verb *esmen*, which is the first-person plural form of the verb *to be*. In much the same way, the English verb *are* tells us that the subject is plural rather than singular. Standing alone, *esmen* would imply its own subject and be translated "we are." In John 10:30, however, the subject is already supplied—"I and the Father" *(ego kai ho pater)*—and *esmen* is used merely to agree with that subject. It simply means "are." Greek has a separate word, *hemeis*, for the pronoun we, but it does not appear in John 10:30. (The entire verse reads, *ego kai ho pater hen esmen.*)

In short, this "devastating" argument from the Greek tells us nothing that we do not already know from the English: "I and the Father" is a first-person plural subject, and the word *one* sometimes bears the connotation of union. We recognize that there is a plurality here— humanity and deity—but not a plurality of persons in the Godhead (John 17:3; I Timothy 2:5). We agree that the man Christ Jesus was fully united with the Spirit of God, but we also understand that the Father was incarnate in Jesus (John 14:9-11).

Finally, the newsletter maintains that "tongue speaking and other phenomena" in the UPCI are actually "counterfeit," saying that the UPCI "imitates modern charismatic or pentecostal revival techniques." How can someone say that the biblical experiences of Oneness Pentecostals are all counterfeit while evidently accepting trinitarian Pentecostal experiences as genuine? How can he explain the thousands of divine healings, manifestations of spiritual gifts, and baptisms of the Holy Spirit in the UPCI, particularly when many people receive the Holy Ghost in UPCI churches before they study Oneness doctrine? If all Oneness tongues speaking is counterfeit, how can thousands of trinitarians receive the Holy Spirit (some of them while in trinitarian churches), subsequently be led to the truths of baptism in Jesus' name and Oneness, and then continue to speak in tongues and enjoy the presence of the Holy Spirit in the same manner as before? Far from imitating modern charismatics, the founders of the UPCI were an integral part of the twentieth-century Pentecostal movement from its beginnings.

Several years ago, Robert Bowman, one of Martin's chief researchers, acknowledged to me in a telephone conversation that most UPCI converts truly have faith in Christ and receive salvation, but he maintained that when they progress in doctrinal study and consciously embrace the Oneness view then they lose salvation. It is an unusual cult indeed that leads people to salvation but then gradually takes it away from them!

Martin not only believes that some UPCI members are saved but also that once a person is saved he can never lose his salvation. This means he is attacking those whom he considers to be fellow Christians and seeking to destroy their churches. It would seem more appropriate to let the Lord of these people decide how to judge these churches and deal with them as He wills, rather than appointing oneself to that role. "Who art thou that judgest another man's servant? to his own master he standeth or falleth. Yea, he shall be holden up: for God is able to make him stand" (Romans 14:4).

Interestingly, Martin's own doctrine of the trinity contradicts one of the most widely accepted formulations of trinitarianism, the Athanasian Creed, which says its teachings are essential to salvation. Although Martin believes in three eternal persons in the Godhead, his book *Kingdom of the Cults* claims, in violation of the creed, that the term *Son* relates only to the Incarnation and does not properly apply to God before that time, and he openly denies the orthodox trinitarian doctrines of the "eternal Son" and the eternal generation of the Son.[1] Moreover, Martin's position on the "eternal Son" contradicts his own more recent use of Proverbs 30:4 to demonstrate a preexistent Son.

Most trinitarian theologians also reject a doctrine Martin propounded in a recent, taped lecture against Jehovah's Witnesses, namely, that the second person of the trinity gave up omniscience, omnipresence, and omnipotence in the Incarnation. This view reduces Jesus Christ to a demigod while He was on earth. For example, in the story of the woman with the issue of blood, Martin cited Jesus' question, "Who touched me?" as evidence that Jesus did not know all things, not understanding that He was asking a rhetorical question for the people's sake. The woman herself realized that she and her action were not hidden from Jesus (Luke 8:47). And on many other occasions Jesus revealed His omniscience (Matthew 9:4; John 1:47-50).

In summary, Walter Martin's explanation of UPCI doctrine and history is clearly erroneous, as someone can readily ascertain by consulting either trinitarian or Oneness sources. His translation of John 10:30 is biased, unwarranted, and misleading. His characterization of the faith and spiritual experiences of UPCI members is a sweeping generalization unsupported by concrete evidence or comparative study. In addition to being unbiblical, his form of trinitarianism deviates from the very standard to which he appeals: church tradition and majority opinion.

The conclusion is inescapable: Walter Martin's attack on the United Pentecostal Church is not credible. At best, it is a case of faulty scholarship; at worst, it is a deliberate distortion.

We can only hope that in the future those who wish to

analyze our movement will approach us with an open mind, state our doctrinal position and history accurately, observe the work of God's Spirit in our churches and lives, and reason with us scripturally. If they do, they will find that, while we do not regard man-made creeds and traditions as authoritative, we are firmly committed to studying, discussing, preaching, teaching, believing, and obeying the Word of God.

Note: In 1989, less than a year after this article was first published, Walter Martin passed away unexpectedly at age sixty. Hank Hanegraaff is the current "Bible Answer Man" and president of the Christian Research Institute, the heresy-hunting organization founded by Martin. Stephen Strang, the founder, editor, and publisher of *Charisma*, has criticized Hanegraaff's methods. Strang wrote in his magazine:

> The heresy hunters are still with us. Only now, instead of stakes, they use their books and radio programs to destroy those they consider heretics. . . . I'm concerned that heresy hunting may be turning into leukemia because some cult-watchers seem more intent on destroying parts of the body than healing the body. . . . Hanegraaff goes way too far [in attacking independent charismatics]. . . . It's time he shows as much respect to fellow Christians with whom he disagrees as he does to those outside the faith.[2]

Appendix B

An Answer to a Critic

Review of Gregory A. Boyd, *Oneness Pentecostals and the Trinity* (Grand Rapids: Baker, 1992).

This book is the first on Oneness Pentecostalism to be offered by a major publisher. The movement's size and historical significance certainly merit a scholarly analysis. This work makes only a modest contribution to an understanding of the movement, however, due to its polemical nature.

The author discloses that at age sixteen he was converted from a life of sin to the United Pentecostal Church International (UPCI), and he embraced the Oneness doctrine. Shortly thereafter he began to question some UPCI teachings. In college, his study of church history convinced him that the Oneness message was erroneous, and he left the UPCI at age twenty. Eventually he became a minister with the United Church of Christ.

The stated purpose of his book is to affirm the third-century doctrine of the trinity and to combat Oneness Pentecostalism. The book concludes that the Oneness view is a "heresy" and "sub-Christian," and indicates that the UPCI may even be a cult.

The author states the basic Oneness doctrine clearly and fairly, using representative Oneness sources. Unlike past attacks by men such as Carl Brumback and Jimmy Swaggart, this book does not misrepresent basic Oneness views or make the erroneous charge of Arianism. More-over, the author excludes a number of popular trinitarian arguments that do not have scholarly validity. This section of the book provides a service by giving readers a generally accurate overview of the Oneness doctrine, although they could easily investigate the primary works for themselves.

In refuting Oneness, Boyd presents standard trinitarian arguments, particularly those of Thomas Aquinas. His biblical points are not new; they are addressed in Oneness works such as *The Oneness of God* (1983).[1] Boyd relies heavily upon ancient church history and philosophical reasoning to prove that trinitarianism is both correct and necessary. He does not utilize, however, the extensive analysis and reflection of significant theologians in this century. He devotes a chapter to asserting that the early postapostolic writers were trinitarian, but curiously, he does not interact with the most extensive Oneness work on this subject, *Oneness and Trinity, A.D. 100-300* (1991), although a copy was available to him. He revives arguments against the ancient modalists—such as the allegation that they had an abstract, impersonal view of God—that do not appear to be relevant to modern Oneness.

Perhaps the strongest chapter of the book is the presentation of scriptural passages that distinguish between the Father and Jesus. This chapter relies on biblical argument, which is the only valid basis for establishing doctrinal truth. This section could help some Oneness believers develop more well-rounded terminology and thought by causing them to consider more seriously the Sonship of Jesus. Yet Boyd does not seem to realize that a distinction between the Father and the Son (not of eternal person-hood, but relative to the Incarnation) is at the very core of Oneness theology, and he does not present the more recent, full-orbed discussion of Oneness authors on this subject.

On other subjects, the author makes a number of un-substantiated, erroneous, and inflammatory charges. For example, he accuses the UPCI of "teaching salvation-by-works to an extent almost unparalleled in the history of Christianity," of teaching "baptismal regeneration," of teaching that a person must be "salvation-worthy" and must "purify" himself to receive the Holy Spirit, of being "the most legalistic 'Christian' movement in church histo-ry," of believing that the trinity is "the most diabolical reli-gious hoax and scandal in history," and of believing that no one holding a trinitarian view is saved.

What prompts these charges is the UPCI's teaching that repentance, water baptism, and the baptism of the Holy Spirit constitute the "Bible standard of full salva-tion," and the UPCI's advocacy of practical holiness teachings such as modesty of dress and women's having long hair.

On these issues the author's bias, limited UPCI expe-rience, and limited research handicap him. He does not interact with major UPCI works on these subjects, such as *The New Birth* (1984) and *Practical Holiness: A Sec-ond Look* (1985), that expressly refute salvation by works, baptismal regeneration, and legalism. Instead he relies on anecdotal examples, secondary works, and unofficial sources, many of which clearly do not reflect standard UPCI views or practices.

In trying to establish that the UPCI is grossly aberrant

on these issues, he does not consider historical and contemporary evidence to the contrary. He does not seem to realize that the UPCI's view of the role of water baptism corresponds closely to that of the first five centuries of Christendom, the Roman Catholic Church, the Eastern Orthodox Church, and the Lutheran Church. He does not consider contemporary works by significant evangelical and charismatic writers, such as Larry Christenson, Kilian McDonnell, James Dunn, and David Pawson, that speak of water baptism and Spirit baptism as part of Christian initiation. And most of his arguments against the baptism of the Holy Spirit would apply to the Pentecostal movement generally.

Boyd does not recognize that the holiness standards taught by the UPCI have been advocated by many ancient writers, Anabaptists, Quakers, Methodists, Holiness groups, Fundamentalists, Evangelicals, and trinitarian Pentecostals. For example, he states that "neither the early church, nor the church throughout the ages, has ever held to the very eccentric notion that a woman should never cut her hair." As *Practical Holiness* documents, however, advocates of women's keeping their hair long, based on I Corinthians 11, include Clement of Alexandria, Tertullian, John Chrysostom, and, earlier in this century, most of the groups mentioned above.

The author clinches his argument by attempting to show that Oneness believers inevitably and almost unconsciously think in trinitarian categories. This assertion seems to undercut his attempt to classify them as heretics or worse, but it does point the way to a more fruitful analysis. That is, if Oneness believers typically express themselves in ways that at least some trinitarians find to be functionally trinitarian, is there more common ground than one might suppose from the tone of this book?

Instead of focusing on philosophical arguments, historical opinions, creedal formulations, nonbiblical terminology, and derogatory labels, perhaps Oneness and trinitarian theologians could profit from a dialogue that could erase some misconceptions, correct some mutual imbalances, and encourage greater attention to a more strictly biblical theology. The difference between Oneness and trinitarianism is more than semantics, yet those who share common spiritual experiences and values may also find some surprising commonalities of thought as well.

Notes

Chapter 1. The Oneness View of Jesus Christ

[1]Tim Dowley, et. al., eds., *Eerdman's Handbook to the History of the Church* (Grand Rapids: Eerdmans, 1977), 619.

[2]See David Bernard, *The Oneness of God* (Hazelwood, Mo.: Word Aflame Press, 1983), 236-54.

[3]See, for example, Isaiah 43:10-11; 44:6, 24; 45:21; 46:9; John 17:3; Romans 3:30; I Corinthians 8:4-6; I Timothy 2:5; James 2:19. Whatever term is used to define God—such as being, nature, substance, or person—it can only be used in the singular; that is, God is numerically one being, nature, substance, or person. Galatians 3:20 says flatly, "God is one"; it does not say, "There is one God [in three persons]."

[4]See *The New Catholic Encyclopedia*, s. v. "Trinity, Holy"; Emil Brunner, *The Christian Doctrine of God* (Philadelphia: Westminster Press, 1949), 236-39.

[5]Scholars generally conclude that I John 5:7 was not part of the original text. In any case, it does not divide Father, Word, and Spirit into distinct persons any more than a man, his word, and his spirit are distinct persons, but it describes the ways God has made Himself known to us. And it concludes, "These three are one." In contrast to verse 8, it does not merely say, "These three agree in one."

[6]Robert Morey, a prolific evangelical author and speaker, used this analogy in a videotaped discussion at the studio of Cornerstone Television in Wall, Pennsylvania, on May 1, 1989.

[7]Finis Dake, *Dake's Annotated Reference Bible* (Lawrenceville, Ga.: Dake's Bible Sales, 1963), NT: 280.

[8]Jimmy Swaggart, "Brother Swaggart, Here's My Question," *The Evangelist*, July 1983, 15. See also idem, "The Error of the

'Jesus Only' Doctrine," *The Evangelist*, April 1981, 6.

[9]See Isaiah 7:14; 9:6; 35:4-6 (with Matthew 11:1-6); Micah 5:2; Matthew 1:23; Acts 20:28; Romans 9:5; II Corinthians 4:4; Colossians 1:15; I Timothy 3:16; Titus 2:13; Hebrews 1:2; II Peter 1:1; I John 5:20. In view of the strong Oneness emphasis on the deity of Jesus, it is misleading to speak of Oneness believers as "unitarians," a term that in both historical and dictionary usage indicates a denial of the deity of Jesus. Likewise, the charge of Arianism is simply false.

[10]Frank Stagg, *The Holy Spirit Today* (Nashville: Broadman, 1973), 17-18, emphasis in original.

[11]See Isaiah 40:3, 5; 45:23; 52:6; Jeremiah 23:5-6; Zechariah 11:12; 12:10; John 8:58; Philippians 2:9-11.

[12]Lewis Smedes, *Union with Christ*, rev. ed. (Grand Rapids: Eerdmans, 1983), 41-54.

[13]Walter Bauer, William F. Arndt, F. Wilbur Gingrich, and Frederick W. Danker, *A Greek-English Lexicon of the New Testament and Other Early Christian Literature*, 2nd ed. (Chicago: University of Chicago Press, 1979), 507.

[14]Bernard Ramm, *Protestant Biblical Interpretation*, 3rd ed. (Grand Rapids: Baker, 1965), 171.

[15]W. A. Criswell, *Expository Sermons on Revelation* (Grand Rapids: Zondervan, 1961-66), 5:42. See also ibid., 1:145-46.

[16]For this reason, Oneness believers today generally reject the label "Jesus Only." The label originally referred to the Jesus Name baptismal formula, not to the Oneness view of God. Its current use by trinitarians is misleading and may reveal a bias.

[17]Henry Thiessen, *Lectures in Systematic Theology*, rev. ed. (Grand Rapids: Eerdmans, 1979), 77.

[18]See Matthew 26:38; Luke 2:40; 22:42; 23:46; John 1:14; Acts 2:31; Philippians 2:5; Hebrews 10:5, 10.

[19]Thiessen, *Lectures in Systematic Theology*, 223.

[20]According to Bauer, et al., *Greek-English Lexicon*, 572-73, *en to onomati* in Acts 10:48 means *"with mention of the name, while naming* or *calling on the name, . . . be baptized* or *have oneself baptized while naming the name of Jesus Christ"*; and *epi to onomati* in Acts 2:38 means *"when someone's name is mentioned* or *called upon,* or *mentioning someone's name"* (emphasis in original). For further allusions to the Jesus Name baptismal formula, see Acts 15:17; Romans 6:3-4; I Corinthians 1:13; 6:11; Galatians 3:27; Colossians 2:12; James 2:7. For further discussion of baptism in the name of Jesus, see David Bernard, *The New Birth* (Hazelwood, Mo.: Word Aflame Press, 1984), 156-85; idem, *In the Name of Jesus* (Hazelwood, Mo.: Word Aflame Press, 1992).

[21]For full treatment of such passages in both testaments, see David Bernard, *The Oneness of God*, 146-235.

[22]Stagg, *The Holy Spirit Today*, 11-12.

Chapter 2. The Word Became Flesh

[1]Oscar Cullman, *The Christology of the New Testament* (London: SCM Press, 1963), 265-66.

Chapter 3. The Almighty God As a Humble Servant

[1]John Miller, *Is God a Trinity?* (By the author, 1876; repr. Hazelwood, Mo.: Word Aflame Press, 1975).

[2]Bauer, et al., *Greek-English Lexicon*, 428.

Chapter 6. The Son of God

[1]F. F. Bruce, *The Epistles to the Colossians, to Philemon, and to the Ephesians*, vol. 6 of *The New International Commentary on the New Testament* (Grand Rapids: Eerdmans, 1984), 52.

[2]Leon Morris, *The First Epistles of Paul to the Corinthians*,

vol. 7 of *The Tyndale New Testament Commentaries* (Grand Rapids: Eerdmans, 1958), 217-18.

Chapter 10. The Right Hand of God
[1]Deuteronomy 33:2; Job 40:14; Psalm 16:8; 17:7; 18:35; 20:6; 21:8; 44:3; 45:4; 60:5; 63:8; 73:23; 77:10; 78:54; 80:15, 17; 89:13, 25, 42; 108:6; 109:31; 118:15-16; 137:5; 139:10; Isaiah 62:8; 63:12; Lamentations 2:3-4; Ezekiel 21:22; Habakkuk 2:16; Acts 5:31; Revelation 1:16.

[2]Bruce, *Epistles*, 132-33. The quote from Martin Luther is from *Werke*, Weimarer Ausgabe 23, 131.

[3]Robert Ross, "The Epistle to the Hebrews," in *The Wycliffe Bible Commentary*, ed. Charles Pfeiffer and Everett Harrison (Chicago: Moody Press, 1962), 1419.

[4]W. E. Vine, *Expository Dictionary of New Testament Words* (McLean, Va: MacDonald Publishing Co., n.d.), 407.

[5]R. V. G. Tasker, *The Gospel According to St. Matthew*, vol. 1 of *The Tyndale New Testament Commentaries*, ed. R. V. G. Tasker (Grand Rapids: Eerdmans, 1961), 176.

[6]Leon Morris, *The Revelation of St. John*, vol. 20 of *The Tyndale New Testament Commentaries*, ed. R. V. G. Tasker (Grand Rapids: Eerdmans, n.d.), 77.

Chapter 11. Whom Will We See in Heaven?
[1]Ramm, *Protestant Biblical Interpretation*, 171.

[2]H. D. M. Spence and Joseph Exell, eds., *The Pulpit Commentary* (Rpt. Grand Rapids: Eerdmans, 1977), 22:162, 165.

[3]Bauer, et al., *Greek-English Lexicon*, 507.

Appendix A. The True Doctrinal Views of the United Pentecostal Church on the Godhead

[1]Walter Martin, *The Kingdom of the Cults* (Minneapolis: Bethany, rev. ed. 1985), 116-17.

[2]Stephen Strang, "Bridge Builders or Stone Throwers?" *Charisma*, August 1993, 14-16.

Appendix B: An Answer to a Critic

[1]All the books mentioned in this review are by David K. Bernard.

Bibliography

For a more comprehensive bibliography see David K. Bernard, *The Oneness of God.*

Bauer, Walter, William F. Arndt, F. Wilbur Gingrich, and Frederick Danker. *A Greek-English Lexicon of the New Testament and Other Early Christian Literature.* 2nd ed. Chicago: University of Chicago Press, 1979.

Bernard, David K. *In the Name of Jesus.* Hazelwood, Mo.: Word Aflame Press, 1992.

_____. *The Oneness of God.* Hazelwood, Mo.: Word Aflame Press, 1983.

_____. *The New Birth.* Hazelwood, Mo.: Word Aflame Press, 1984.

_____. "Oneness Christology." In *Symposium on Oneness Pentecostalism 1986.* Hazelwood, Mo.: United Pentecostal Church International, 1986.

Boyd, Gregory. *Oneness Pentecostals and the Trinity.* Grand Rapids: Baker, 1992.

Bruce, F. F. *The Epistles to the Colossians, to Philemon, and to the Ephesians.* Vol. 6 of *The New International Commentary on the New Testament.* Grand Rapids: Eerdmans, 1984.

Brumback, Carl. *God in Three Persons.* Cleveland, Tenn.: Pathway Press, 1959.

Brunner, Emil. *The Christian Doctrine of God.* Philadelphia: Westminster Press, 1949.

Criswell, W. A. *Expository Sermons on Revelation.* 5 vols. Grand Rapids: Zondervan, 1961-66.

Cullman, Oscar. *The Christology of the New Testament.* London: SCM Press, 1963.

Dake, Finis. *Dake's Annotated Reference Bible.* Lawrencevilee, Ga: Dake's Bible Sales, 1963,

Dowley, Tim, et. al., eds. *Eerdman's Handbook to the History of the Church.* Grand Rapids: Eerdmans, 1977.

Martin, Walter. *The Kingdom of the Cults.* Rev. ed. Minneapolis: Bethany House Publishers, 1985.

Miller, John. *Is God a Trinity?* By the author, 1876. Reprint. Hazelwood, Mo.: Word Aflame Press, 1975.

New Catholic Encyclopedia, The. New York: McGraw Hill, 1967.

Pfeiffer, Charles, and Everett Harrison. *The Wycliffe Bible Commentary.* Chicago: Moody Press, 1962.

Ramm, Bernard. *Protestant Biblical Interpretation.* 3rd ed. Grand Rapids: Baker, 1965.

Smedes, Lewis. *Union with Christ.* rev. ed. Grand Rapids: Eerdmans, 1983.

Spence, H. D. M., and Joseph Exell, eds. *The Pulpit Commentary.* Reprint. Grand Rapids: Eerdmans, 1977.

Stagg, Frank. *The Holy Spirit Today.* Nashville: Broadman, 1973.

Strang, Stephen. "Bridge Builders or Stone Throwers?" *Charisma.* August 1993.

Swaggart, Jimmy. "The Error of the 'Jesus Only' Doctrine." *The Evangelist.* April 1981.

———. "Brother Swaggart, Here's My Question," *The Evangelist.* July 1983.

Tasker, R. V. G., ed. *The Tyndale New Testament Commentaries.* 20 vols. Grand Rapids: Eerdmans, 1961.

Thiessen, Henry. *Lectures in Systematic Theology.* rev. ed. Grand Rapids: Eerdmans, 1979.

Vine, W. E. *Expository Dictionary of New Testament Words.* McLean, Va.: MacDonald Publishing Co., n.d.

Scripture Index

Subject Index

oneness: of believers, 95-98; of Father and Son, 95-109; of husband and wife, 101-2
Oneness Pentecostals and the Trinity, 149-53

Pawson, David, 152
Pentecostals, 144, 152
person, persons, 11-12, 13, 15, 36, 66, 78, 87-88, 91, 96, 106, 127, 136-37
Peter, 60, 67
Philip, 99-100
Philo, 35
philosophy, 35,150
Pilate, 128
plural references to God, 25-26, 52-54
polytheism, 27, 53
prayers of Christ, 26-27, 89-90, 95
preexistence of Jesus, 75-77, 115-16
Presbyterians, 44
Protestants, 143
Pulpit Commentary, 137

Quakers, 152

Ramm, Bernard, 15, 136
redemption, 16, 61, 82, 86, 132
Resurrection, the, 113-14
right hand of God, 28, 119-27
Roman Catholic Church, 143, 152

salvation, 30-31, 89-92, 114, 145, 151
Samaritan woman, 10, 35
Savior, 30-31
Sheba, queen of, 131
Smedes, Lewis, 14
Solomon, 131
Son, 14, 15-19, 27, 38-39, 55-57, 67-83, 91, 105-9, 111, 141-42, 150-51
Southern Baptist Convention, 15
Stagg, Frank, 12-13, 26-27